FEAR OF A "BLACK" AMERICA

FEAR OF A "BLACK" AMERICA

✦

Multiculturalism and the African American Experience

Donald Earl Collins

iUniverse, Inc.
New York Lincoln Shanghai

Fear of a "Black" America
Multiculturalism and the African American Experience

iUniverse, Inc.

For information address:
iUniverse, Inc.
2021 Pine Lake Road, Suite 100
Lincoln, NE 68512
www.iuniverse.com

ISBN: 0-595-32552-1

Printed in the United States of America

To Harold I. Meltzer and Barbara A. Lazarus,

for bringing light to my path in some of my darkest days

Contents

Preface

Sometime around 1998, the intellectual world considered the American "culture wars" a dead issue. "Multiculturalism is dead," many critics essentially said. The need to create a more inclusive curriculum and build a more inclusive society no longer inspired interest. The media and the publishing world took the hint, and now seldom show enthusiasm for this once hot and controversial topic.

The events following 9/11 have bolstered the claims of many intellectuals, in that we are in an age where displaying our xenophobia is acceptable. Racial profiling—whether of Blacks or Arab Americans—is a necessary good. Americans currently live in fear, the talking heads say, and this fear justifies the suspension of the entire Bill of Rights.

The underlying meaning of these events is that multiculturalism is more relevant than ever, and that the "culture wars" are not over. How could they be? What that tragic day in the Northeast proved was that our capitalist culture had little grasp of the level of desperation with which those from outside the U.S. would act. They acted in retaliation for our nation's economic and cultural imperialism, both real and imagined. Certainly their actions cannot be justified, but how can we stop these terrorists if we do not attempt to understand their perspective, however twisted?

How can multiculturalism be irrelevant if at the time of the attack only a couple of FBI agents (out of about 7,000) possessed a grasp of Arabic, though Arabic is one of the five most spoken languages in the world? Our domestic security agencies had done little to recruit Arab Americans or Arabic speakers despite heightened concerns about Osama bin Laden and the strategic importance of the Middle East to daily American life.

Is multiculturalism irrelevant when media outlets such as FOX and the *Washington Post* allow gigantically one-sided discussions between pundits and politicians about the need to profile young Arab-looking men (and occasionally women) to assuage American fears? Profiling our fellow citizens is okay, the talking heads say, because Americans—especially White Americans—desperately want to feel safe. It is precisely this kind of thinking that requires multiculturalism as a philosophy in American culture.

Two weeks after 9/11, *Time* Magazine published a cover story titled "Why Do They Hate Us?," as if the entire Muslim world was responsible for the attack and merely jealous of America's material wealth. If we possessed a greater concern for culture than educator E.D. Hirsch's super-Anglo ramblings about it, *Time* would not have needed to title a cover article with such a biased question.

Our nation's response to 9/11 suggests that if we as a multicultural people continue to allow the usual suspects of politicians, pundits, and publishers to speak for us, then the culture wars truly are over. And those who hold dearly to xenophobia, racism, and the Anglo in American culture will be the victors. Regardless of how much fear we as multicultural Americans possess, rejecting multiculturalism in a multicultural society will continue to have disastrous consequences.

For well over a decade, I have interviewed, researched, and presented to the point of nausea about multiculturalism and its relationship to the African American experience. Some folks have been willing to grant that multiculturalism has an address in the history and culture of African Americans, standing as an alternative to assimilationist and separatist movements. But given that, I have also seen many scholars and public intellectuals respond in what I can only interpret as fear and skepticism toward it. Fear in that the philosophy would lead to the downfall of so-called high culture (meaning Anglo-American cultural dominance) in American society. Skepticism in that these "other" cultures have contributed little of significance to the development of America's cultural fabric, nor should they be expected to in the future. I can only conclude that the fundamental issue here is the fear of educators, the media and the press, and political leadership of losing their place of presumed dominance.

I truly hope that Americans Black, White, Latino, Asian, Arab, Native, Christian, Muslim, Jewish, straight, and LGBT can overcome their fear and skepticism toward the non-Anglo in our collective American tapestry. Multiculturalism must take a central place in American life if we ever hope to see this otherwise great nation live up to its democratic ideals of freedom, equality, and opportunity. Otherwise the grand experiment known as America will continue to fail. But it will not fail because of other terrorist attacks, militia groups or race riots. Failure will be assured as long as fearful Americans allow the powerful to exploit them. America must choose the difficult yet rewarding path of faith in its ideals and peoples if we ever expect to overcome this fear of a multicultural America.

Introduction

"Multiculturalism" arises as a reaction against Anglo- or Eurocentrism; but at what point does it pass over into an ethnocentrism of its own? The very word, instead of referring as it should to all cultures, has come to refer only to non-Western, non-white cultures.

—Arthur M. Schlesinger, Jr., The Disuniting of America, 1992.

What is pure? Who is pure?/Is it European state of being/I'm not sure…
Excuse us for the news/I question those accused
Why is this fear of Black from White/Influence who you choose?

—Public Enemy, "Fear of a Black Planet," 1990.

It was in my History of American Education class at Duquesne University during the 1998–99 year that several of my graduate students raised objections to the teaching of "extreme multiculturalism" in America's public schools. I had given these current and future teachers Arthur Schlesinger Jr.'s *Disuniting of America* (1992) to read as part of a paper assignment, thinking that they would be able to ascertain the differences between assimilation, Afrocentricity, and multiculturalism. Before they read Schlesinger, I had also provided my students with definitions of these terms. I was surprised to find that only a couple of my students had considered my definitions in comparison to Schlesinger's. Most saw multiculturalism and Afrocentricity as two names for the same thing: ethnocentrism. One student even argued that cultural pluralism (which is used interchangeably with the term multiculturalism) was "good" while multiculturalism was destructive and "evil."

I then asked the class what I thought was a simple question during our Schlesinger discussion: Who or what is an "American?" No one could give me a definitive answer. What happened instead was that my students recited several American ideals such as free speech, democracy, hard work, individualism, and equality. I pointed out exactly what Schlesinger insists in his book; that these ideals are what *should* hold all Americans together as one culture, but part of what makes America unique is the right to disagree and disagree loudly. Like the words of the Ku Klux Klan and neo-Nazi groups, the First Amendment allows the expressions of Afrocentrists, and any attempt by Schlesinger or anyone else to eliminate this form of cultural debate in American education would be contradicting part of what it means to be an "American." I think this caveat caused a few of my students to more closely interrogate Schlesinger's fast and loose use of multiculturalism in reference to Afrocentricity. It did not, however, cause them to stop addressing African Americans and other persons of color as "them," "they," and "minorities," and themselves as "us," "we," and "Americans." This occurred in an all-White class, one in which nearly all of the students hoped to teach in predominately White suburban school districts

Far from a critique of my students, this example illustrates what my students and many other Americans are fearful of when it comes to multiculturalism. Schlesinger's ultimate fear in *Disuniting of America* is the "Balkanization of America" as downtrodden non-Western and non-White peoples force multiculturalism down the throats of the ruling Anglo-Americans and their honorary "Anglo" adoptees. What is Schlesinger's solution to stopping the "cult of ethnicity?" As Public Enemy puts it, Schlesinger wants to keep the "European state of being" pure, even though one can easily contend that it has never been as pure as Ivory Soap. Certainly not in the American context, as Englishmen, American Indians, and Africans have been in a state of physical and cultural interaction since 1619.

So why the title *Fear of a "Black" America*? Because, as Barbara Ehrenreich's title *Fear of Falling* also denotes, there is a fear among many Americans that non-Western/non-White peoples and their cultures will eventually overrun the Anglo-dominated American culture as their numbers swell and their voices grow louder. The ones who benefit most from an Anglo-centered culture stand to lose the most, not only in terms of power, but also in terms of identity. To be sure, Public Enemy's "Fear of a Black Planet" refers to how Black "genes and chromosomes" threaten Whites and the fear that Black men would choose White women as mates for the purposes of eradicating White America. So the title *Fear of a "Black" America* alludes to a fear of losing control over American culture to African Americans, Hispanic Americans, Native Americans, Asian Americans (among other non WASP and male groupings), with the influence of Black culture as the ultimate manifestation of this fear.

But this trepidation is more than just the realization that the Anglo-centered American culture is under attack from the barbaric non-Whites. Besides the feeling of apprehension, we can also define fear as the absence or a lack of faith. What this means is that many Americans opposed to multiculturalism are operating under the assumption that America was never meant to include peoples of color and their non-Western cultures, when in fact (and in spite of itself) American culture has always been a blend of different cultures. Many Americans simply do not believe that African Americans and other people of color are capable of deciding on their own how to be "American" while maintaining their non-Anglo essence. Those opposed to multiculturalism as an American cultural or educational philosophy believe that their "American" heritage must remain forever unchanged, because any attempts at meaningful inclusion would destroy their own understanding of what it means to be an "American." In other words, a multicultural America in terms of *philosophy* and demography creates a lack of faith on the part of many White Americans. Many have little faith in their "American" identity (based on assumptions of superiority) surviving on a level playing field—a fear of falling.

The problem with the absence of faith is that this results in the projection of fear in all of its manifestations onto those who had little to do with the formation of the fear in the first place. In other words, if knowledge gives one power—and if cultures convey knowledge to its participants—then part of this fear stems from the assumption that non-Whites will gain power and wield it in ways Whites have over people of color in the past. White fear of multiculturalism, Afrocentricity, and non-White cultures is really a lack of faith among White Americans that the American tapestry can explicitly include the supposedly inferior fabrics of peoples of color without ripping apart. Unfortunately, Schlesinger, my students, historians, educators, and most Americans regardless of race/ethnicity do not understand how fluid culture is, especially in the American context. From food to music to clothing to ideas, the vast majority of Americans work with popular cultural idioms that the Founding Fathers did not account for in the Constitution or the Bill of Rights. One should not assume, however, that White Americans as a whole would want to share cultural (and therefore general) power in any meaningful way with African Americans and other people of color beyond the search for "proper representatives" among them.

At the same time, racism, discrimination, and those good-old American values of free speech and individualism (for both groups and individuals) have enabled non-mainstream cultures to survive in an American context. To assume that Afrocentricity is bad because it will destroy our one, big, happy American family suggests that: 1) America has always been a united country culturally; 2) that African Americans and other groups (including White Americans) are monolithic; and 3) that non-Whites are so stupid that they will follow anyone whose ideas sound better than assimilation as a means to wash off their inferiority. Even if every African American decided to adopt an Afrocentric philosophy, Blacks only make up between twelve and thirteen percent of America's population. America would not be plunged into a culture (read "race") war because of Afrocentricity. The reality is, however, that African Americans are as individual and diverse as American society's collective whole.

Some African Americans and other peoples of color, on the other hand, faithfully believe that Whites will never really attempt to share political and cultural power with them. Afrocentricity and similar cultural movements among non-Whites exist partly because of disenchantment with an Anglo-dominated America. These movements represent a fear of cultural and/or literal extinction as a result of Western cultural dominance.

Multiculturalism has been hurt by the advent of Afrocentricity as a philosophy for Black empowerment and as a strategy for raising African American educational achievement. Following in the traditions of Black nationalism and separatism dating back to Martin Delany, Marcus Garvey, and a pre-1963 Malcolm X, Afrocentricity appears on its face to be similar to multiculturalism. Both philosophies promote the idea that the African American experience has been fundamentally important to the development of American society. This is probably where the similarities end, as most proponents of Afrocentricity are primarily concerned with the ancient African experience contained in the civilizations of ancient Egypt (or Kemet), Songhai, Mali, and Timbuktu.

The majority of Afrocentrists are interested in the African American experience only for the purposes of justifying their belief that Western culture is one that degrades Blacks and other people of color, is destructive in its core nature, and offers nothing that would liberate the hearts and minds of African Americans. The African American experience is also useful as a straw man to hold up in contrast to the salvation proposed by Afrocentricity, with its beliefs in Black unity and its almost complete delegitimization of anything perceived as Western or "White." This includes everything from rock 'n' roll to religion, from Brahms to the Bible, and from caffeine to capitalism. Becoming a true believer in Afrocentricity requires recognizing the limits of Western culture and American society for Blacks, and necessitates Blacks suing for a divorce from many things Western and "White."

Of course Afrocentricity scares White Americans because of its staunch views of American society and because it advocates Black independence from it. If one ever decided to take a poll of African Americans, a fairly large percentage would probably also say they are apprehensive about the implications of Afrocentricity. Fear of Afrocentricity goes beyond the philosophy, however, because scholars such as Schlesinger have tied it up with the more appealing multiculturalism. One should also note that proponents of Afrocentricity on the local and national levels have received significantly more media attention than anyone in the business of promoting multiculturalism. In the past decade, Afrocentrists such as Molefi Asante and Leonard Jeffries have become much more well known than, say, James Banks. The media's treatment of Black America as a monolithic whole feeds into the idea that all African Americans really do believe in the idea of Afrocentricity, and the result of this feeds into the fears of White America.

But Afrocentricity and its nationalist/separatist predecessors do more than simply scare Whites, cause scholars who are against multiculturalism to use Afrocentricity as a straw man to be confused with multiculturalism, and enable most Americans to see Black Americans as monolithic in thought. It also allows many African American scholars who may or may not be Afrocentrists—and White scholars of the Black experience—to view Black thought as either monolithic or in constant bipolar opposition. For conservative Black scholars such as Thomas Sowell and Roger Wilkins, the Black community represents a collage of pathologies that only serve to increase the problems of advancement, and believe that Blacks must become "Americans" (i.e., White) in order to leave their cultural pathologies behind. For equally conservative Afrocentric scholars like Asante and Jeffries, Blacks must become more "African" in order to break free of the American chains that bind them. While neither camp describes African Americans as merely victims, both negate the complexity of what we call the Black community in terms of thought and vision.

There is yet another group of White and Black scholars, perhaps the majority, who believe that there have only been and remain to be two camps of African American thought, one that believes in assimilation or integration, the other placing their faith in nationalism or separatism. For many scholars, multiculturalism could not have existed as a concept among African Americans simply because the isolating effects of segregation and exclusion from much of the American mainstream would not have allowed Blacks to think much beyond black or White. So many consider any promotion of the African American experience by African Americans in any time period in American history as the drive of some Blacks toward nationalism and separatism. And with the rise of Afrocentricity over the past two decades, many scholars of the Black experience would argue that the nationalist/separatist strain among African Americans remains strong. Those Blacks who are advocates of assimilation and integration are perceived to be "Uncle Toms" who are in the minority, and some Black scholars treat them as such. Is it any wonder that if many African American scholars do not see their counterparts possessing a number of perspectives about Black thought and the direction of Black America, then why would the rest of America?

In any case, there is some resistance among scholars of African America to the idea that there is a lot of gray between the views of people like Clarence Thomas and Louis Farrakhan, or even between Jesse Jackson and Tony Brown. The common argument made against the involvement of African Americans in the development of multiculturalism, however, is that the promotion of the Black experience as worthy of praise by African Americans must somehow fit the general mold of Black nationalism. The problem with that argument is that it puts such luminaries as W. E. B. Du Bois, Carter G. Woodson, Marcus Garvey, and Malcolm X in the same box with no major distinctions between them. Yet the general view is that whenever there has been an upsurge of interest by Blacks in the African American experience, it must be part of a wave of Black nationalism.

Without a doubt the counterarguments of many scholars of the Black experience against the possibility of multiculturalism among African Americans for any time period include: 1) "Well, multiculturalism was not even a word until recently, so how could any African Americans have practiced it?;" 2) "There's no way that ordinary Blacks could have even conceived the notion of multiculturalism in any time period, because they were too busy trying to survive to think of such things;" and 3) "Even if one grants the possibility that multiculturalism as a concept existed in American society well before the word did, this term could not possibly describe the activities of African Americans with regard to their group experiences and those of Whites. That's biculturalism, not multiculturalism." The only answer to those charges that I can give here is that they are rooted in the belief that the activities of both Blacks and Whites are relatively easy to sum up, almost to the point where even academicians can treat both Black and White America as monolithic.

What makes it so difficult for many scholars to accept the idea that the Black community's leading intellectuals and ordinary members of Black America could engage in activities that might lend themselves to multiculturalism? Part of this stems from the reality that the term itself is loaded with an array of connotations beyond its literal meaning of "many cultures." Another piece in this puzzle comes from academicians (particularly but not exclusively Black ones) who are also operating in fear. Certainly this "fear" is not literally of the Black experience or community itself, but it is based on having to make a significant paradigm shift. Not only would one have to acknowledge the fluidity of culture, but the role of multiculturalism would complicate much of what scholarship understands as Black thought on assimilation and separatism. In short, the fear for scholars in this case is of history being revised into myth, warping the Black experience in the process.

Which again brings us back to the larger fear of cultural collapse among many Americans, White, Black, and other people of color. White American fear of multiculturalism—which is a lack of faith in the American tapestry's ability to hold together while making a concerted effort to include the experiences of non-Whites—can only be dealt with by eradicating this "miseducation" hidden in the verbiage of pseudo-scholarship. Defining terms like American, multiculturalism, Afrocentricity, and assimilation would give scholars and laypersons alike a better understanding of what really is at stake regarding American culture, not the misinformation that multiculturalism will be American culture's eventual downfall.

Schlesinger's pronouncements regarding multiculturalism and Afrocentricity are scary not because multiculturalism and Afrocentricity are either good or evil, but because Schlesinger's fear has led to the miseducation of many otherwise open-minded Americans. The faith of Afrocentrists in the evils of Western culture and glories of ancient Egypt has also skewed the minds of many Americans regardless of color against multiculturalism. And the faith of much contemporary scholarship in their rendering of Black America as monolithic and Black thought as a duality of opposition does nothing to promote a deeper understanding of the African American experience and America's multicultural past. It is the purpose of this book to evaluate multiculturalism in a different light, a light of faith and truth, rather than one of apprehension and accusation.

Part One: Fear and Multiculturalism

1

Fear of a "Black" America and Multiculturalism

Ask the average American or even the typical American historian how to define multiculturalism, and one might elicit any number of ambiguous responses. One person might say, "Gee, I don't know...Why are you asking me?" Another rugged individualist could say "Multiculturalism?!?...That word makes me think of bleeding-heart liberals who want America to favor the Blacks and other minorities!!" An elementary school teacher would probably remark that "Multiculturalism is like a Barney the Dinosaur song, 'I love you, you love me,...'" The typical American historian might boldly declare that multiculturalism "represents a series of sociocultural processes that originated with urbanization and industrialization during the Gilded Age and culminated with the invention of the Internet." An expert on multiculturalism should count themselves lucky if a person answering their question can say "Hmm...'multi' means many, so I guess multiculturalism means the study of many cultures."

Given this lack of understanding of the term multiculturalism, it would seem as if advocates would face little opposition to its usage. Unfortunately for the American public, long-winded and unproductive debates have surrounded the subject of multiculturalism ever since it became a major educational and political issue in the 1980s. Everyone from Diane Ravitch to William Bennett to Pat Robertson and the 700 Club has a negative opinion of multiculturalism, calling it "divisive," "particularistic," and "tribal," but few have actually attempted to define it. Multiculturalism's proponents, meanwhile, use definitions that enable other educators and academics to understand its usefulness in America's schools, but they have not been able to communicate their research to the American public.

This study is designed to take a long, hard look at what multiculturalism means and its development among African Americans during the last century.

There are those who would argue that Blacks could not have participated in multiculturalism's development until recent years. Other so-called experts (along with a host of average Americans) believe that African Americans have only developed ideas such as nationalism/separatism and desegregation/integration since the end of slavery. It must be said that these arguments assume that Blacks have been and remain too narrow-minded, dumb, or preoccupied with Jim Crow, crime, and survival to seriously consider their place in society beyond "Back to Africa" movements and Martin Luther King, Jr's "I Have A Dream" speech. Based on the aforementioned definition, many elite and non-elite Blacks have practiced multiculturalism on some level, if only because circumstances forced the issue upon them.

A dramatized popular culture example of this was an exchange that occurred on the television series *Law & Order* between characters played by actors Sam Waterston, Courtney B. Vance, and Wendell Pierce. Vance (Black) portrayed an arrogant Wall Street stockbroker named Benjamin "Bud" Greer. Waterston (White) played the role of Manhattan Assistant District Attorney Jack McCoy. McCoy indicted Greer for murdering his White boss, while Greer—whose defense was based on the theory that "Black rage" caused him to murder his boss—attempted to justify his defense to McCoy by claiming that he was forced to live in a White-dominated world of discrimination and dehumanization. Wendell Pierce (Black) played Greer's defense lawyer and insisted that if McCoy wanted to, he "could spend [his] entire life without any significant contact with a Black man." But if "Bud" Greer, on the other hand, "didn't want to mix with the White man, he would have to remain in Harlem or Bedford-Stuyvesant or South Central Los Angeles." Greer also felt that he *had* to lick the boots of his White boss and White co-workers every day in order to advance in his life—this was what allegedly caused Greer to snap. The point here, in any case, is that many African Americans believe that they have to participate in mainstream American culture in order to advance in American society. This does not necessarily mean assimilation, but rather, having a multicultural understanding of themselves and others in the diverse and divided world known as America.

Multiculturalism As A Process of Discovery:

What many Americans have failed to understand is that multiculturalism has existed in American society from the moment native Americans, Europeans, and enslaved Africans began to interact. For native Americans, enslaved Africans, and other peoples of color, this interaction has produced a need to understand others' cultures and how their own cultures would enable them to adapt to the dominant one. It is not just about the total number of "groups" (i.e., racial, ethnic, religious, cultural, etc.) involved in the process of cultural interaction. Multiculturalism fundamentally is a process of discovery, whether for oneself, a group, or the interaction of several groups.

My own process of discovery began on Wednesday, September 9, 1981 as a seventh grader at the A. B. Davis Middle School in Mount Vernon, NY, a suburb outside New York City. Not only was this the first day of the 1981–82 school year, but it was also my first day in the Mount Vernon Public Schools' Humanities Program. Over the next three years, my life would be influenced by my participation in this program.

Between September 1981 and June 1984, I faced ridicule and harassment from my classmates, friends, and neighbors over my beliefs, my relative lack of preparedness for the "creme de la creme" program I entered, and because of my family's working-poor background. Five months before the start of seventh grade, my mother and ex-stepfather exposed me to the Hebrew-Israelite religion, which meant that we believed that we were "Black Jews." The Jewish, Italian, and African American students could not understand how I knew I was "Jewish," especially since I had never visited Israel. Nor did they comprehend why I insisted on wearing Jewish clothing such as a kufi (a multi-holed skullcap for everyday wear and worship) and a yarmulka. From what I can remember, one Italian student decided that my kufi looked like clams on-the-half-shell, so he called it a "kufi on-the-half-shell." I guess that it would have been interesting if my kufi actually tasted like clams on-the-half-shell, but that probably would not have been "kosher."

Many Black and White students deliberately labeled my yarmulka a "Yamaha," including those enrolled in the Humanities Program. Teachers and administrators who were primarily of Italian or Jewish descent attempted to prevent me from wearing my kufi or yarmulka by taking it off of my head or threatening to expel me from school. They also poked fun at the fact that a Black student thought he was "Jewish" and therefore "White," or told me that they did not understand why my parents thought it was necessary for me to be so open about my beliefs. I was involved in several fights because students from A. B. Davis Middle School and Mount Vernon High School would try to steal my kufi or yarmulka off my head. Classmates and neighbors who had been my friends in elementary school no longer acknowledged my presence. I also discovered that many of the students enrolled in the Humanities Program thought that I was inferior to them because I had not been in the Program as long as they had (some students started as early as the second grade) and because I did not wear more expensive and fashionable clothes. It did not help that I grew from five feet, four inches tall in seventh grade to six feet tall during ninth grade; my feet also grew from a size nine and a half to a size thirteen. These religious and physical differences only enhanced my awkwardness with the student population, especially since most of my classmates were nurtured in more "traditional" Jewish and Christian households, and since I towered by at least six inches over the majority of them. I realized even then that my situation was unusual, that I was unusual, but I did not want to concede this to my spoiled and bratty classmates precisely because I was afraid that it would embarrass me and my family.

The Humanities Program introduced me and my classmates to two unique courses in the ninth grade: Afro-Asian History and Afro-Asian Literature. The history and literature classes examined the development of the Middle East, Egypt, Sub-Saharan Africa, India, China, Japan, and Asian Russia. Both classes allowed us to learn about these cultures from the point of view of the people who lived in them. Our teachers also exposed us to various belief systems stemming from Afro-Asian cultures through our studies and actual attempts of interaction. These belief systems included Paganism, Hinduism, Islam, Buddhism, Confucianism, Animism, Judaism, and comparisons with Christianity.

While many of my classmates seemed only mildly interested in other cultures and religions at best, I used what I learned as part of my decision to no longer claim that I was a Hebrew-Israelite. These classes opened my eyes to a world I knew relatively little about, even though my parents (mostly my ex-stepfather) expected me to believe that everything I needed to know was between Genesis and Deuteronomy. I began to think consciously about what I believed and why because I felt that the belief system they had taught me lacked a real and intimate connection to God and to me. I literally compared and contrasted the different religions we learned about in class not only to obtain an academic understanding of them but also to see if any of them could give me a sense of who I was in relation to God. Of all the aforementioned belief systems, I concluded that Christianity brought me closest to understanding God, myself, and other groups without significant prejudice or bias. I also concluded that historical circumstances linked a number of major world religions, which somehow led me to believe that Christianity was the right spiritual path for me to follow. I eventually decided to become a Christian, and did so by the end of ninth grade. In spite of my ex-stepfather and about 200 confused administrators, teachers, and classmates, I changed from who I was into who I decided to become. As a young, Christian, African American male living in metropolitan New York in 1984, I felt as if I had finally discovered myself. I also realized as a result of these classes not only that different groups—for a variety of geographic, cultural, and historical reasons—possess different belief systems, but that there was a great diversity of thought even within the same belief system, especially in the case of Christianity. In the end, this process was my first true experience with multiculturalism, which probably would not have happened without the unconscious cooperation of the Humanities Program.

What disappointed me about how the Humanities Program and the Mount Vernon school system implemented this multicultural classroom experience was that they did not give other students a chance to take these classes. In a school system that was more that seventy percent Black, and more than eighty percent Black and Hispanic, the Humanities Program was about sixty percent White during the mid-1980s. In fact, Mount Vernon High School and the rest of the school system became increasingly Afro-Caribbean (i.e., Jamaican, Barbadian, Haitian), Hispanic, and Asian by the end of the decade. Yet, only students who were part of the Program could take such advanced courses as Afro-Asian history and literature in ninth grade. Most of these students came from affluent White and African American families, and were able to increase their educational advantages with these multicultural classes. Mount Vernon school board members and the Humanities Program administrators apparently designed it to cater to privileged White students and the middle and working-class Black students whose parents either wielded some political and economic influence in the city or were lucky enough to have caring teachers and administrators who helped them into the Program. Evidence of this was the Mount Vernon Board of Education's plan which phased out the Humanities Program from the school system in the early-1990s, as many upper middle class White parents removed their children from an overwhelmingly non-White school population.

It would have made sense to introduce the courses that the Humanities Program offered to the entire student population, particularly to the poor, working-class, and lower middle class African American, Afro-Caribbean, Hispanic, and Asian students. For the poor and persons of color are much less likely to travel extensively, to visit museums, and to meet other groups outside their immediate environment. Multiculturalism in public schools such as Mount Vernon would enable these students to be more aware of the world beyond their neighborhoods, and would make them more aware of their place in the world, perhaps even their purpose for living. Without this program and the Afro-Asian classes specifically, my interest in understanding others would be minimal, and I would not have a clear understanding of my place in this world.

Defining Multiculturalism:

Certainly self or group discovery is an initial motive or catalyst for a multicultur-alist outlook, but most people and most groups do not consciously attempt to gain an understanding of other groups. **Part of what defines multiculturalism is the cultural reality resulting from diverse groups *interacting* in a variety of equal and unequal relationships over several generations.** This is because a multicultural society by definition is a volatile, dynamic, interactive one, and is not bound by theoretical models that are only expected to work in the post-industrial 1990s or in the midst of mainstream scholarship. Any notion of multi-culturalism that *does not* acknowledge the fluidity of culture in the American con-text assumes that because American culture is based primarily on Western ideology, that "other" cultures have a limited or secondary function in American society. These assumptions, moreover, are elitist, and devalue the contributions that other groups and cultures have made to the pillars of American society. Mul-ticulturalism is more than just various groups of people *learning* about diverse cultures. Multiculturalism is about various groups of people *discovering* who they are through a critical and oftentimes complex examination of their own and oth-ers' cultures.

While almost everyone thinks that they possess the agreed-upon definition of multiculturalism, the reality is that most mistake it for assimilation or American-ization. Multiculturalism does involve the process of absorbing the social and cul-tural values of Anglo-American society. True assimilation cannot occur, however, unless a person has already gained an understanding of their own culture.

Multiculturalism and Related Concepts			
	Multiculturalism	**Assimilation**	**Afrocentricity**
Definition	*a philosophy and practice allowing groups who interact to discover who they are through a critical and oftentimes complex examination of their own and others' cultures.*	*a philosophy that believes fundamentally in "One America." Regardless of race, ethnicity, gender, class, religion, all must somehow conform to a White, Anglo-Saxon, Protestant, and male view of the world.*	*a philosophy that emphasizes the African American and especially African experience, particularly of pre-1492 African kingdoms. This philosophy generally assumes that Western culture is inferior to ancient African cultures because of Eurocentrism 's issues of dominance.*
Related Terms	***a.k.a.:*** *Pluralism, Cultural Pluralism, Multicultural Education.* **Related to:** *Intercultural Education, Womanism, and Afrocentricity.*	***a.k.a.:*** *Americanization, notions of the "Melting Pot" and "Salad Bowl."* **Related to:** *Integration.*	***a.k.a.:*** *Africentricity, Afrocentrism, Black Studies, Africana Studies.* **Related to:** *Black Nationalism, Pan-Africanism, and Multiculturalism*
History	*First use of "cultural pluralism" came from Harvard instructor Horace Kallen in 1906. Rachel Davis-DuBois, Alain Locke and James Banks, have expanded on Kallen's ideas.*	*Became prominent in the late-19th century with mass immigration to the U.S., as elites sought to "melt" these groups into the "pot" of American ideals while purging their inferior cultures.*	*Movements promoting African culture date to the mid-19th century. Ones most relevant include the 1920s Garvey movement and the 1960s and 1970s rise of Black Studies. Advocates include Molefi Asante and Leonard Jeffries.*
Use in Education	*Meant to change the way subjects (especially in the humanities) are taught by including the people and the contributions of people of color in school curricula.*	*Civics/English-only classes were created by educators to "Americanize" immigrants between 1890 &1940. William Bennett, Diane Ravitch, and Arthur Schlesinger argue for a return to "American" values.*	*First introduced in Black Studies departments during the 1970s, then adapted for some predominantly Black school districts during the 1980s and 1990s to bolster self-esteem and Black achievement.*

I could not have concluded, for instance, that Christianity was right for me if the Humanities Program had not initially exposed me to some rudimentary tenets of other belief systems. Multiculturalism involves elements of assimilation, self and group identity, and empowerment on the basis of education. These same elements can come together to form multiculturalist ideas when a *group* begins to discuss who they are, how they can understand the dominant society in order to succeed despite it, and what concepts or strategies would enable them to overcome any forms of prejudice and discrimination, regardless of the time period.

What is NOT Multiculturalism:

Although multiculturalism contains elements of what scholars have termed "melting pot" theory, bicultural education, and bilingual education, all three have been attempts to assimilate non-dominant cultures into a Western-dominated American culture. "Melting pot" theory, otherwise known as assimilation or Americanization, is the antithesis of multiculturalism; it uses the existence of non-Western cultures to proclaim the superiority of Western culture. Whether one was Black, Native American, Italian, Jewish, Japanese, or Polish, the notion of a melting pot would essentially "melt" these groups into Americans. In the case of the "melting pot" theory, being American meant accepting the values of Western Europe and Anglo-America: capitalism, the Protestant work ethic (if not Protestant Christianity), and the English language. Developed as a phrase and theory in 1908, the notion of the "melting pot" had dominated the curricula of American public education until the 1970s.

Bicultural education refers specifically to the cultural exchange of *two* different groups, and assumes that White Americans, African Americans, Hispanic Americans, Asian American, and native Americans all have one unified culture. Given the relative fluidity of culture (particularly popular culture) in American society—not to mention the differences within groups because of class, religion, language, and point of origin—it would be next to impossible to argue that bicultural education is the equivalent of multiculturalism. Bicultural education, bilingual education, and intercultural education were offshoots of the "melting pot" theory, so educational programs based on them, no matter how innovative, heralded Western culture's superiority.

For the same reason, Marcus Garvey's "Back to Africa" movement of the 1920s and his Universal Negro Improvement Association (UNIA), the emergence of Afrocentric education, and other Pan-African movements would also be incompatible with multiculturalism. Although Garvey's activities involved large numbers of rank-and-file African Americans, they either proclaimed the moral superiority of African/African American cultures, or promoted Western culture as intellectually superior (as in the case of Garvey). Even with its roots in multiculturalism, Afrocentric education asserts that Western culture is inherently inferior to African (particularly ancient African) cultures.

Afrocentricity as a philosophy is typically misconstrued as multiculturalism or a form of education that would threaten to divide American society along racial lines. Instead, Afrocentricity provides a vehicle for analysis relevant specifically to the African and African American experience—particularly in the areas of history and cultural studies—for African Americans. Afrocentricity essentially is a derivative of both the Black Studies movement that began in the late-1960s and multiculturalism. While the Black Studies movement also insisted that universities address African/African American history and culture in their curricula, it did not have the same impact on the curricula of public schools.

Afrocentricity is a popularized conception of education for African Americans meant for consumption in all public institutions which African Americans participate, including public schools. Although many Black Studies programs have held an essentially Afrocentric paradigm since the late-1960s, Afrocentricity has only become popular among Blacks outside of the university in the past two decades. Molefi Asante (the so-called "Father of Afrocentricity"), Leonard Jeffries, Asa Hilliard, John Henrik Clarke, and Maulana Karenga are among the growing number of African American scholars and intellectuals who have popularized it. Asante's publication of *The Afrocentric Idea* (1987) played a key role in encouraging African American educators to think seriously about implementing Afrocentric curricula in the public schools.

Since 1985, in fact, a number of school districts across the United States have adopted some version of what could be described as Afrocentric curricula for their Black students. Portland, Oregon, Atlanta, Milwaukee, Detroit, Baltimore, and Washington, D.C. are among the school districts who have led the charge for curricula that centers the experiences of African Americans. Included in this implementation process since 1989 have been Black male classrooms, justified by the argument that African American males have even more specialized needs for development and maturation than their female counterparts.

Beginning in the late-1980s with California and New York's attempts to revise its history curricula for their public schools, conservative scholars and educators like William Bennett and Thomas Sowell have sharply flayed Afrocentricity as "unscholarly," "divisive," and "exclusionary." Scholars such as Diane Ravitch and Arthur Schlesinger have gone as far as to label Afrocentricity "multiculturalism" in order to maintain a sort of cultural canon status quo. Liberal scholars have also critiqued Afrocentricity for its almost total concern with ancient Egypt and its polemic dismissal of Eurocentric education and knowledge.

A Theoretical Framework for Multiculturalism:

Although education is the primary vehicle of multiculturalism that I examine here, multiculturalism entails more than remedies derived from education and educational institutions. Multiculturalism can also refer to a movement by any group of people to control the process of cultural creation and maintenance in their own communities in the midst of a dominant mainstream culture. This was true of both first-generation Italians in America in 1900 and of African Americans during the same time period. As American cultural historian Lawrence Levine said, "[a]udiences...come to popular culture with a past, with ideas, with values, with expectations, with a sense of how things are and should be." Blacks certainly must have examined their own and the larger society's culture critically in creating strategies for the community's success. The Black sociocultural historian Robin D. G. Kelley went further, suggesting that what the mainstream culture regards as part of its own canon other groups (including African Americans) interpret as "authentically" belonging to their own cultural constitution. As a result, a contest for cultural maintenance and an erosion of cultural differences takes place in the multiculturalism process.

The popularization of hip-hop/rap culture among African Americans and its proliferation among other groups—including many White Americans—is a most recent example of multiculturalism at work beyond schools. Pioneering hip-hop/rap artists have given credit to people from Barry Manilow and John Denver to George Clinton and The Last Poets for their musical development. At the same time, some of these artists want to keep their music "hard" or "real," meaning they want their music to remain as authentically "Black" as possible. White Americans and other groups, meanwhile, have become more fascinated with hip-hop/rap culture over the past fifteen years, to the point where some identify with cutting-edge nationalist group Public Enemy, while others are intrigued with gansta rappers Dr. Dre and the late Tupac Shakur. Some Whites (like The Beastie Boys, Eminem, and House of Pain) are hip-hop/rap artists themselves or are self-proclaimed "wiggers" (an adaptation of the "N" word for Whites) who are "keepin' it real." Multiculturalism, in this commodified form, has not only benefitted non-dominant groups like African Americans culturally, but also has been absorbed for the financial and entertainment benefit of many in mainstream America.

One must also acknowledge the impact of differential socioeconomic and political power inside/outside the Black community on the historical development of multiculturalism. Perhaps the reason desegregation became the battle cry of African Americans from the late-1930s into the 1960s in the midst of multiculturalist activities was because Black elites (scholarship and leadership)—and, more broadly, mainstream America—saw desegregation as a strategy that would most quickly and effectively put Blacks on an equal footing with Whites. This is not to say that many prominent African Americans refused to support multiculturalism, nor that the African American working-class generally opposed desegregation. What it does say is that we must take intrarace relations into account in order to understand multiculturalism in the context of desegregation from the 1930s through the 1960s.

Multiculturalism as Strategy for African Americans:

Strategies for Black educational empowerment influenced and were influenced by the demographic transformation of the community and urban environment and the distribution of resources among Black and White schools. African American scholars and leaders who were involved in changing the nature of education for their brothers and sisters reviewed what African Americans were taught in schools, the number of Black teachers in the public school system, and the makeup and distribution of Whites (and funds) in school systems. African American scholars and leaders of the first half of the 20th century assumed that a closer *physical* proximity of African Americans to Whites would lead to a generational breakdown of racial barriers in the hearts and minds of Whites and a drive to desegregate public schools. The difficulties with desegregation and integration stem from little consideration of *cultural* proximity in the desegregation strategy.

This definition of desegregation—meaning the opening up of opportunities for Blacks to obtain the same educational, job, housing, public services, and political entitlements guaranteed to Whites—is different from how we generally define desegregation today. Desegregation has come to mean "wanting to be White" to many African Americans, and certainly some who fought for an end to segregation might very well have wanted all the trappings of Whiteness. Some scholars, in fact, draw a distinction between desegregation and integration; desegregation was the method by which America would become an integrated society. Desegregation was not an end in itself, but a way in which African Americans could become fully American. Integration, on the other hand, was the culmination of Blacks becoming more American and less African or "other." For better or worse, desegregation and integration have become loaded terms, reviled by Blacks and Whites alike as concepts which allowed prominent African Americans to take on the psychological and financial trappings of Whiteness.

For similar reasons, I have also chosen to use the terms "Black" and "African American" interchangeably throughout the book. Although "Black" does not come into general use until the late-1960s—and "African American" until the late-1980s—"Negro" and "Colored" are loaded with all kinds of historical and contemporary connotations, and would make the story of this book a confusing one. Despite the nationalist origins of the more contemporary terms "Black" and "African American," my purpose for using both is partly as a literary device, demonstrating the multicultural nature of African America.

Distribution and demographic strategies, in any case, took precedence over other strategies to alleviate African American problems in education and in American society at large. A concern for giving African Americans the same legal civil rights as White Americans superseded strategies that emphasized changing the substance of education for African Americans in order to ensure legal, economic, political, and social equality for future generations. Multiculturalism represented an alternative to desegregation.

The African American intellectual elite developed their notions of multiculturalism and desegregation as strategies for race uplift during the late-1920s and through the 1930s. By the 1930s, migration, the Harlem Renaissance, the Depression, and the failure of Booker T. Washington's industrial education and W. E. B. Du Bois' "Talented Tenth" programs impacted the ideas of the Black intelligentsia in Washington and elsewhere. During this period, Black intellectuals such as Du Bois, Alain Locke, Carter G. Woodson, and Anna J. Cooper wrote in support of multiculturalism, desegregation, and the combination of the two as strategies to uplift Blacks.

Like other African American elites, many in the Black Washington intelligentsia saw themselves as better than the rest of the community. In some ways, they viewed their lives and careers as more comparable to their White counterparts than to other, non-elite Blacks. While it is not clear whether the Black Washington elite perceived themselves as American first and Black second, many in the Black intellectual elite had bought into the melting pot notion that Anglo-American culture was superior to the African American experience. This was probably not a deliberate action on their part; "melting pot" theory definitely played a part in their thinking between the late-1920s and 1954.

It is important to realize that for the pre-1954 period, while not all leaders were intellectuals, almost all intellectuals expected to take a leadership position in the community. A number of historians have noted the innovative and important function that African American intellectuals played, particularly before the *Brown* decision. It should be no surprise that their prevailing educational, cultural, and overall race strategies inevitably impacted the organizations that these intellectuals participated in and oftentimes led, including the NAACP, historically Black colleges and universities (e.g., Howard University, Morehouse College, and Spelman College) and segregated public schools.

Demographic changes and an inequitable distribution of resources in segregated public schools also affected how Black teachers taught their students, primarily in informal ways. With an increasing number of Black students, few new buildings to house them, and no provisions for a formal curriculum that catered to Blacks, African American teachers found it possible to only discuss issues of race in the classroom on an informal basis. Although Negro History Week (the third week in February) existed throughout the mid-twentieth century in Black Washington, this was only one of several ways Black teachers attempted to "instill race pride" in their students. Through plays, dialogue, and strong ties between parents and teachers, the principles of what we currently call multiculturalism were taught to Black children (regardless of class) in conjunction with the formal, mainstream-American-centered curriculum.

Multiculturalism: Does It Have A History?:

The term multiculturalism raises some conceptual problems when viewed from a historical perspective. African Americans did not use the term multiculturalism to describe the cultural and educational theory that developed during the 1920s and 1930s. Although one of the first public uses of the term "cultural pluralism" (a term often used interchangeably with multiculturalism) by a Black intellectual came in a speech by Alain Locke in 1924, Black scholars and educators in the 1920s and 1930s were generally not concerned with multiculturalism from the perspectives of gender, class, and religion. For African Americans, multiculturalism has involved negotiating the difficult terrain of Black history, Black actions against American racism, and mainstream, Anglo-American culture. African Americans, in other words, have not only used multiculturalism as a *philosophy*, but also as a *strategy* for race advancement and as a means of educating Blacks about their own identity and experience. The basic principles from which multiculturalism has developed, in any case, were much the same even when the concern centered only on race.

A number of early-20th century African American intellectuals anticipated the development of multiculturalism in African American communities. Du Bois' oft-quoted section from *The Souls of Black Folk* (1903) is a clear example of mul-

ticulturalism as it is defined here. Noting that it is "a peculiar sensation, this double-consciousness, this sense of always looking at one's self through the eyes of
others," Du Bois was attempting to find a way to mold double-consciousness into
a positive sensation for Black advancement. According to Du Bois biographer
David Levering Lewis, *Souls of Black Folk* "transcended" any previous debate
about defining African Americans through assimilation or separateness "by
affirming [this dichotomy] in a permanent tension...[of] proud, enduring
hyphenation." Du Bois understood that in spite of the tremendous cultural and
psychological damage that African Americans bore as a result of slavery and the
rise of Jim Crow, that Blacks retained a measure of their African essence (or
"Africanness") while believing themselves to be fully American (at least culturally). Du Bois believed that African Americans could take advantage of their
simultaneous interaction with—and separateness from—American culture by
taking pride in their uniqueness and putting it to work to better the race.

In a speech to graduating Howard University students in 1930, Du Bois
argued that the "university education of Black men in the United States must be
grounded in the condition and work of those men!" The Black university should
also seek "from a beginning of the history of the Negro in America and in Africa
to interpret all history; from a beginning of social development among Negro
slaves and freemen in America and Negro tribes and kingdoms in Africa, to interpret and understand all mankind in all ages." Three decades after *Souls of Black
Folk*, Du Bois continued to push for African Americans to gain a fuller awareness
of their African and American essences.

Carter G. Woodson, the "Father of Black History," outlined a plan that
sought the uplift of African Americans through an education oriented toward the
African American experience in the early-1930s. Woodson suggested that key
institutions in the African American community (e.g., schools, churches, community centers) must become enlightened and oriented toward "their people
rather than away from them." Woodson also stressed the study of anthropology,
history, and sociology from the point of view and for the purpose of ameliorating
African American social ills.

Carter G. Woodson addressed multiculturalism in a more specific way than
Du Bois in his *Mis-education of the Negro* (1933). Woodson contended that
Blacks should not "**spend all their time** in advanced work on Shakespeare,
Chaucer, and Anglo-Saxon," but should "direct their attention also to the folk-
lore of the African [emphasis added]" and African American writers. To be sure,
Woodson wanted Black leaders, scholars, and teachers to be "reeducated" in the
African/African American experience. Unlike proponents of Afrocentricity,

Woodson was not arguing for an education based solely on African and African American history and culture, for he believed that this would be an "unwise course." Woodson's emphasis here was to right a wrong—the exclusion and warping of the African American experience from the American public school curriculum—not Black nationalism. This is why Woodson believed that African Americans should not "spend *all* their time" studying an Anglo-dominated curriculum; they should, however, spend *some* of their time understanding the majority/dominant culture. Interestingly, other groups such as Italians or Jews are rarely accused of ethnocentrism because they place some emphasis on understanding their histories and cultures. African Americans, in contrast, are consistently labeled as "militant," "nationalistic," "racist," and "Afrocentric" for pushing the inclusion of the African American experience within the context of an Anglo-centered curriculum. In short, Du Bois and Woodson both argued for multiculturalism as a race-based strategy of cultural and educational uplift.

The late Black cultural historian Nathan Huggins argued in *Harlem Renaissance* (1971) that Black intellectuals such as E. Franklin Frazier and Alain Locke saw this period as one where "Negro life is seizing upon its first chances for group expression and self-determination." Multiculturalism for African Americans grew out of years of discussion and confrontation among scholars and the larger community over the kind of education and type of strategy that would uplift the African American community.

Alain Locke's work is also consistent with the way I define multiculturalism here and the way African American intellectuals have made use of the concept. Locke, in fact, was one of the first intellectuals to encounter and use multiculturalism's parallel term cultural pluralism. Locke picked up the term firsthand as it originated from a class at Harvard taught by the then teacher assistant Horace Kallen in 1906. Much of Locke's academic work from the mid-1910s until his death in 1954 dealt with issues of race uplift, cultural empowerment, and what would now be called intercultural or multicultural education. In a 1916 lecture titled "Racial Progress and Adjustment," for instance, the Harvard-trained Black philosopher noted that

> [t]he group needs, in the first place, to get a right conception of itself, and it can only do that through the stimulation of pride in itself. Pride in itself is race pride, [and] the very stimulation to collective activity which race pride or racial self-respect may give will issue into the...common standard.

Locke suggested that an environment that encouraged race pride—both in the African American community and in American society—would enable African Americans to become full members of American society while maintaining their own cultural identity. Du Bois, Woodson, and Locke all concluded that the Anglo-dominated American culture would have to include and appreciate America's Black voices if the idea of America was to survive at all.

Fear of a "Black" America is an attempt to provide an explanation of a term and a philosophy that politicians, pundits, and educational policymakers have argued about for the past two decades. The book should enable readers to realize that many writers and speakers on multiculturalism have misled many Americans into believing that even saying the word is tantamount to blasphemy. This is also the story of African Americans who—contrary to popular American opinion—were intelligent, disciplined, and desperate enough to attempt to find ways to conquer discrimination, dehumanization, and fear.

2

Heady Days: African American Intellectuals and Multiculturalism

There was a time in my life when I was desperate to publish an article in a scholarly journal. My reasoning was that it would help me obtain an academic position, raise my status as a historian, and enhance my chances of publishing a book. I could not have been more off base. I found out how wrong I was at an informal meeting with two editors from an education journal in March 1998. I had submitted an article for publication with this journal twelve months earlier, and had made several revisions at the request of the senior editor. He had served as my professor for a graduate class in the spring of 1992. Over the course of a two-hour so-called lunch, he and his assistant grilled me about the contents of my article, my writing in general, and about the publishing business. Now I knew that this essay would need more revisions, but a two-hour inquisition on why a 28-year-old is too young to make bold conclusions based on existing studies made little sense.

Among other things, the editors commented that I was too young to write an essay that reviewed previous scholarly work in Black history, education, and multiculturalism. Their logic: "even a senior scholar with fifteen years in the field would have trouble pulling this off." The editors also insisted that the only road to academic Nirvana regarding my work would be through publishing academic articles and books that met the approval of an exclusive scholarly community. Translation: "write something that is interesting to a few other professors—but not so exciting that it would catch the public's attention—and by all means do not work on something as controversial as multiculturalism." Publishing a book with a reputable scholarly press was the editors' ideal regarding my future, for their assumption was that only a university press could raise the status of an academic manuscript. And we all know what people say about assumptions.

The most irritating comment made by these two editors, however, had little to do with their myopic view of the publishing world or of their hubris regarding the Ivory Tower. The editors insisted that some of the sources I had cited in my article—especially of Black scholars such as Harold Cruse, Robin D. G. Kelley, and Carter G. Woodson—needed the enhancement of White academics like Philip S. Foner and the late August Meier. Foner's little-known essay on Carter G. Woodson's work and its relationship to the American labor movement, if I had used it as a source, would have somehow improved the content and tone of the essay. Having Meier personally review my work (even though he was already in bad health) would have also made my essay a better one.

Although I certainly have no objections to using scholarship produced by Whites in any academic context, these arguments seemed ridiculous to me at the time. The last time I checked, Cruse, Kelley, and Woodson were all ground-breaking historians in African American history. Considering Foner's productive career in Black and labor history, and Meier's prestigious work in African American history (which I had cited in my article), I thought that their comments were also insulting toward them because I doubt that either Foner or Meier would want to be used in this way. Yet if I had made use of Foner and Meier the way the editors believed I should have, it would have made all the difference in the world.

What does this meeting have to do with this chapter? Mainly that in spite of the mountains of solid and oftentimes cutting-edge research produced by African Americans and other people of color, there remains an attitude in academia that Whites must validate this work. This is especially true of work that seems unorthodox or controversial, which could describe Cruse's, Kelley's, or Woodson's scholarship. Why else would two editors approach me about an article's specifics that they would never publish? The editors could easily have rejected my article without any further correspondence or dialogue if this was simply a case of submitting a terrible essay. But there was another kind of fear factor here, not necessarily of race, but of delegitimizing previous White scholarship on African Americans and multiculturalism.

The aforementioned story is important because a sort of scholarly segregation between the work produced by African American and White scholars persists. The importance of mid-twentieth century Black scholarship remains largely obscure and the story of what influenced this intellectual production remains mostly untold. Many academics (Black and White) also have a difficult time believing the extent to which these intellectuals could have developed multicultural ideas.

In the case of prominent African American scholars such as Woodson, W. E. B. Du Bois, Carter G. Woodson, Alain Locke, and Anna Julia Cooper, a dialogue did occur on the question of race advancement through cultural enhancement during the 1920s and 1930s. At conferences, in speeches, and through books, these scholars, intellectuals, and educators communicated on the need for African Americans to gain a fuller understanding of their experience. At the same time, they wanted Blacks of all backgrounds to obtain a more complete comprehension of American society in general and of Whites specifically. Some Black intellectuals, including Du Bois and Locke, also noted that neither Black nor White culture was monolithic, which is why this dialogue is a multicultural one. This chapter's goals are to highlight African American intellectuals and their multicultural ideas, and in the process give them the praise and the examination they deserve.

Defining the Relationship Between Multiculturalism and Desegregation:

At first glance, one would think that multiculturalism and desegregation are indirectly linked ideas at best, or contradictory at worst. Consider, however, the similarities between multiculturalism and desegregation as *strategies* rather than the long-term goals of some supporters. Desegregation's purpose was to eliminate legal barriers to the physical presence of African Americans in exclusively White neighborhoods, schools, jobs, and public facilities. On a physical and legal basis, desegregation was intended to level the playing field for Blacks who were equipped to advance in mainstream American society. Multiculturalism can be seen as the cultural extension of desegregation, in which whatever cultural barriers to understanding racial similarities, differences, and contributions could be eliminated through putting mainstream and non-mainstream cultures on an equal playing field.

One should also consider the time period being examined here. The mid-twentieth century (particularly the 1930s) was the key period for the development of desegregation as a strategy for Black advancement. African American intellectuals, elites, and lawyers were hard at work developing strategies to end legal segregation long before the landmark *Brown v. Board of Education* decision (1954). The 1920s and 1930s are the years which immediately precede World War II and the large-scale efforts to desegregate the U.S. military and American society after the war. This is a key period for an examination of the relationship between multiculturalism and desegregation as strategies.

Yet many other Black elite leaders, educators, and intellectuals would have seen multiculturalism as another threat to their social and cultural hegemony within the Black community. The African American historian Willard B. Gatewood claimed in his *Aristocrats of Color* (1990) that elite Blacks of the late-19th and early 20th centuries "held steadfastly to the hope...of being assimilated in the larger society." While desegregation might have seemed a radical strategy to some Black elites and most Whites, it also seemed more reasonable than the Black nationalism displayed by the followers of Marcus Garvey or of Black Marxists. It would not take a quantum leap of logic to recognize that multicultural ideas would fall under the category of being too radical for many Black elites. Desegregation would enable Black elites to achieve the larger goal of assimilation into mainstream American society, enabling them to take advantage of their education and social status gained during the Jim Crow era.

The Black elite primarily consisted of mostly light-skinned doctors, lawyers, ministers, teachers, professors, government employees, bankers and businessmen during the first two decades of the twentieth century. By mainstream American standards, one would define the Black elite as lower middle class or solidly middle class in terms of income and net worth. But their educational attainment (in many cases at least a bachelor's degree) and social status (skin complexion and family name) made them elite because so few African Americans possessed these trappings in the early twentieth century. By the early-1920s, however, the complexion of the Black elite began to change—literally and figuratively—to include some of the darker-skinned descendants of emancipated slaves, sharecroppers, and domestic workers. The combination of better access to education and the migration of many African Americans to various parts of the urban North and South helped to expand the Black elite. These new inductees diversified the Black elite's ideological base to include not only Booker T. Washington's philosophy of self-help, but also the ideas of "race pride" and emphasis on African/African American culture characterized by the Harlem Renaissance/New Negro movements of the 1920s and early-1930s.

Booker T. Washington, born into slavery in 1856, became infatuated with the idea of vocational training for African Americans while a student at Hampton Institute in Virginia in the late-1870s. Washington established the Tuskegee Institute (now Tuskegee University) in Alabama in 1881 to provide the kind of education he had received at Hampton. Nicknamed the "Wizard of Tuskegee" for his authoritarian control over his school, Washington began to outline a program of economic thrift and self-help for all African Americans during the 1880s and 1890s. Washington thought that in light of increasing Jim Crow segregation, exclusive rights to sharecropping and debt peonage, and state-endorsed violence directed toward Blacks, it was necessary for Blacks to become economically self-sufficient before doing anything about their lack of political power. As Washington described it in his book *Up From Slavery* (1899), gaining economic power in that present time would lead to obtaining political power in the future. Many Black elites steadfastly held to Washington's ideas even after his death in 1915, with the additional component that African Americans should also make themselves culturally compatible to Whites. This would make it easier for Blacks to obtain economic and political power in America. Ward Connerly, among other prominent African Americans, is an ideological descendent of Washington. Connerly, of course, led the recent and successful battles to repeal affirmative action in California and Washington State.

W. E. B. Du Bois' notion of the "Talented Tenth"—as detailed in his *Souls of Black Folk* (1903)—stood in direct opposition to Washington and his supporters. Du Bois argued that Washington's notion of political accommodation (which made Washington an "accommodationist") and economic self-sufficiency was unworkable because one needed political power to protect economic interests. Du Bois believed that the most talented of African Americans (namely, the elite) needed broad-based, college-level training to become the civic and social leaders of the race. That training would help the elite in their fight for political power to protect Blacks from lynch mobs and economic exploitation, because one cannot become rich if one is dead or unable to vote. Vestiges of Du Bois' model remain at prominent Black colleges and universities such as Howard University in Washington, DC, and Morehouse and Spelman Colleges in Atlanta.

With the New Negro movement and the Harlem Renaissance period of the 1920s and 1930s came the idea that the promotion of African American culture was a key factor in the group's advancement. Many elite Blacks believed that sharing culture with other Blacks and with Whites would break down the barriers of segregation and would lead to assimilation. Of course, not all supporters of the New Negro movement and the Harlem Renaissance believed in assimilation, as many supported the celebration of the Black experience as distinctive from mainstream America. This by definition made some of these intellectuals separatists or nationalists. And yet there were African American elites and intellectuals who believed that the combination of possessing race pride, fighting to end segregation, and gaining an understanding of White America would lead to race advancement. This, in turn, would give Blacks the *choice* of assimilation, separatism, or something in between.

These ideological changes among African Americans and within the Black elite occurred not only between West 110th and West 145th Street in Manhattan, but also in other geographic pockets of Black cultural development. According to the great Black philosopher and native Washingtonian Alain Locke, the "New Negro" originated from within the hearts and minds of African Americans, not from a specific geographic location." This would mean that other centers of African American intellectual and cultural activity also participated in the Harlem Renaissance, even if their "Harlem" was the Shaw District of Northwest Washington, the Hill District of Pittsburgh, or the West End section of Atlanta. These developments also fueled a transition period for African American elites in which the old idea of the elite being in charge of the community's moral maturation clashed with a developing new Black elite who wanted to create economic self-sufficiency and cultural self-respect for themselves and everyday African Americans.

Depression, Multiculturalism, and African American Scholars:

For many African Americans (especially in the rural South), the Great Depression began long before the Stock Market Crash of 1929. Between 1925 and 1929, agricultural modernization, the dropping price of cotton and other produce, and farm foreclosures all began to take their toll on Black farmers and sharecroppers. The reality that America's urban centers could not suffice as heaven for African American migrants from the depressed South did not fully set in until 1929.

What was already a difficult mix of economic stagnation, discrimination, and exploitation grew even worse between 1929 and 1935. By the time Franklin D. Roosevelt was sworn in as President in March 1933, the national unemployment rate for African Americans stood between fifty and sixty percent, more than double the overall jobless rate. Even Roosevelt's initiatives to stimulate the floundering economy hurt Blacks at first, as White officials throughout much of the South denied Blacks access to government financial relief. Federal agricultural subsidies (granted under the Agricultural Adjustment Act) enabled White landowners to evict more Black sharecroppers, as the subsidy's purpose was to curtail crop overproduction and keep crop prices from falling even further. In most major U.S. cities, Blacks were the last hired and first fired for even the worst of jobs. If there was any period that generated a variety of fears shared across racial lines, this one was it. Whites were afraid that Blacks would take "their" meager jobs and "their" valuable resources, while African Americans were fearful of starvation and White lynch mobs.

W. E. B. Du Bois:

Enter W. E. B. Du Bois, without a doubt the single most important Black intellectual—some would argue *American* intellectual—of the twentieth century. Du Bois is also one of the least understood intellectuals in American history, even with all the authors who have studied his life and his research. David Levering Lewis' Pulitzer-Prize-winning, two-volume biography of *W. E. B. Du Bois* (1993, 2000) only begins to capture the man's seemingly contradictory thoughts on segregation, Marxism, Black patriotism, Marcus Garvey, the NAACP, and Booker T. Washington. Part of the reason for this is because of Du Bois' biological and intellectual longevity and his varied interests in sociology, history, philosophy, literature/poetry, economics, political science, and religion.

What would come to define Du Bois as an intellectual and an elite activist for years to come was his examination of *The Souls of Black Folk* (1903). Included in his analysis of what lay in store for Blacks in the twentieth century was Du Bois' belief that Booker T. Washington's philosophy of political inaction and economic reaction to segregation was deeply flawed. Du Bois thought that Washington's philosophy would keep African Americans tied to sharecropping and agricultural production without the intellectual of technological tools necessary for economic advancement, much less political or cultural success.

At the Howard University commencement ceremony in 1930, Du Bois delivered a speech in which he noted that Washington's method failed because it could not "foresee changes in the world." Washington's ideas depended on the limited funds given by White philanthropists who were only interested in creating a surplus labor force, not a skilled and educated one. Du Bois also suggested that African American colleges and universities were performing inadequately in training the "Talented Tenth" in the three decades between *The Souls of Black Folk* and the Great Depression. This inadequate training was in the area of economics, specifically how to cope in a rapidly changing industrial society in which Blacks made up the bottom rung of the American Jacob's Ladder.

For Du Bois, his idea of a talented Black elite leading the group to equality—and Washington's opposing view that economic advancement for rural Blacks was the key—had both been made moot by the Great Depression. As Du Bois put it, the Washington-Du Bois struggle of the early-twentieth century "appears merely as a vague legend." This statement is an exaggeration, for there were still Black elites in 1930 who would end business relationships and friendships over whether Washington's or Du Bois' strategies for racial equality was the better one. But Du Bois understood that for many African American elites and for most ordinary Blacks, the Great Depression was proof that these strategies could only work for Blacks who were in the social, economic, or educational positions necessary to take advantage of them. In terms of today's debate over affirmative action, this realization would be something to consider before accusing Blacks of stealing jobs from Whites (specifically White males).

Du Bois' economic foresight regarding Washington's philosophy was not the only idea that began its development in *The Souls of Black Folk* and continued into the 1930s. Du Bois' *Souls of Black Folk* was also one of the first attempts to examine multiculturalism's potential as a vehicle for race advancement and as an answer to the so-called "Negro question." It was also Du Bois' attempt in making it "possible for a man to be both a Negro and an American without being cursed and spit upon by his fellows." Du Bois' discussion of the African American inner-self set him apart from nineteenth century Black leaders like Alexander Crummell, Henry Highland Garnet, Martin Delany, Frederick Douglass, and Booker T. Washington. What makes *Souls of Black Folk* such a special and unique contribution to our understanding of African Americans (and Du Bois) is that Du Bois applied his studies of philosophy to his historical and sociological research. He moved beyond opinion and what could have been a mere study of the "Negro problem" to create a literary masterpiece with multicultural implications.

Du Bois recognized that the history of African Americans had been one of struggle between two inner selves, one African and one American, and that it was a must for these selves to merge into one better self. The African American soul was one in which neither the African nor American essence would be lost in the merger. As Du Bois described it, the African American soul would wish for

> neither of the older selves to be lost. He would neither Africanize America, for America has too much to teach the world and Africa. He would not bleach his Negro soul in a flood of White Americanism, for he knows that Negro blood has a message for the world.

Commenting on Du Bois' examination of the double-consciousness (or dual identity) of African Americans, Lewis suggested that Du Bois was ahead of his time by at least a decade. By the 1920s, artists, writers, and intellectuals across racial lines would express their dissatisfaction with assimilation and mainstream American culture. Du Bois' examination of the war within the souls of Black folk between an African and an American essence was earth-shattering and showed the wisdom of a prophet. According to Lewis, Du Bois must have reached the conclusion that the "Negro self…would become in time and struggle stronger for being doubled, not undermined." Certainly Du Bois' contemplation as stated in the questions of "Am I an American or am I a Negro?...Can I be both?" was a consideration of how African Americans could acknowledge both their "African-ess" and "Americaness" in the process of advancing in American society.

Du Bois' epiphany can be seen in several different ways. One could interpret Du Bois' conception of the African American soul as the ramblings of a madman, because African Americans either perceive themselves to be Black or American, but not both. This perspective would only show that one has missed the point of Du Bois' exercise, not to mention a lack of understanding of African Americans. One could also argue that Du Bois' ideas were about the "twoness" of African Americans, meaning that his ideas have little at all to do with multiculturalism. This would be a misinterpretation of Du Bois' philosophical perspective, for even Du Bois would acknowledge that the African and American essences are not each one solid mass but are both made up of a variety of complicated parts.

There are only two ways, ultimately, to view Du Bois' ideas in this instance. One might suggest that Du Bois' based his statement on his fears, a fear of assimilation, a fear of White violence and hatred strong enough to murder African Americans both physically and culturally. One may also think that Du Bois was reacting to Black self-hatred, a hatred powerful enough to tear the African American soul apart and rendering both African Americans and America culturally useless to the world.

On the flip side, Du Bois could have very well been writing out of faith, a faith in the African American past and how their parents, grandparents, and great-grandparents survived and transformed themselves and America despite the hell of slavery. One can conclude that Du Bois was fully persuaded that the African American spirit—once reconciled by African Americans—would enable Blacks to succeed at and survive anything, including Jim Crow segregation, the slavery of sharecropping, and venomous White violence. Du Bois believed that this process was one which Blacks could only perform for themselves. At the same time, Du Bois placed faith in the American experiment—especially in its positive and negative relationship to African Americans—and believed that Blacks would advance because they were a unique people and made America unique.

By the time of his commencement address at Howard University in 1930, Du Bois recognized that it might be time to put his ideas into action. His speech was mostly a contemplation of strategies to combat the crisis of the Depression, general racial oppression, and a rise in White-on-Black violence. What Du Bois presented to the Howard Class of 1930 was a strategy that would combine Booker T. Washington's perspective on vocational education and economic advancement with his own ideas for providing a liberal arts education for the Black elite. Du Bois contended that a college that joined Tuskegee Institute's curriculum with Howard's would be in the best position to successfully prepare African Americans for the modern world. He also believed that the way to do this would be through a thorough selection process (testing) for "Black men and women of ability," and through providing those African Americans full tuition scholarships. A comprehensive Black college or university could afford to do this because its range of services could attract African Americans from a variety of backgrounds.

Du Bois wanted Black colleges not only to merge and become more comprehensive, but also to become self-sufficient. This was because Du Bois understood that the White philanthropy provided to Black colleges and universities typically came with strings attached, especially in dictating the kind of curriculum an institution could promote. In the past, White philanthropists had given money almost exclusively to Black colleges that promoted Washington's brand of education, while African American liberal arts institutions struggled to find sufficient funds. This kind of education would go beyond Du Bois' notion of the Talented Tenth, for it would allow non-elite African Americans to attend college based on merit rather than family reputation. It would also enable African Americans students to gain the knowledge necessary to establish Black footholds in the American economy, in American politics, and in American culture. Du Bois declared that Blacks will only be able to break down barriers to economic, political, and cultural advancement through "outthinking and outflanking the owners of the world today who are too drunk with their own arrogance and power successfully to oppose us."

The most obvious point Du Bois wanted to make was that if African American higher education was going to survive the Depression, then Black colleges and universities could no longer depend on the half-hearted support of White philanthropists. But there is much more to Du Bois' declaration than this. Du Bois had concluded that African American economic advancement and the reconciling of the Black soul were interconnected issues because of Marcus Garvey's efforts through the Universal Negro Improvement Association (UNIA) to empower working-class Blacks and the Depression's illumination of America's economic fallibility. For Du Bois, the merging of the African and American essences could occur over time, but would happen more quickly and easily through the merger of strategies for Black advancement. A comprehensive African American college that could teach Blacks about American capitalism while providing substance for the African American soul would pave the way for Black advancement in America and Black acceptance of a multicultural soul.

Equally as important was Du Bois' realization of the need for a new African American "elite." Why else would he suggest that the Black college develop a broad-based educational agenda, one based on merit through an examination process, and propose that these students be given full scholarships to attend college? Du Bois understood that the vastness of African American problems made it necessary to overhaul Black higher education. To do that, one would be forced to demolish the elitism rampant in the lofty circles of the African American Ivory Tower. Selecting students based on skin tone (the lighter, the better), family name and profession, and income were all more important than academic, leadership, or personal potential. An elite based on merit would be significantly larger than Du Bois' earlier vision of a Talented Tenth, and would have the advantage of a diversity of experiences to contribute to Black success. African Americans could be "Black" and be "American" through higher education in all of its formal and informal manifestations. Du Bois' 1930 Howard speech was multiculturalism at its core, combining the practicability of Black higher education with the need for cultural and economic power. Du Bois' presentation can also be linked to the movement among elite White universities during the 1930s and 1940s toward standardized testing as the means of selecting students (elite and nonelite) and creating a new, more diverse elite based on ability, as described in Nicholas Lemann's *The Big Test* (1999).

Du Bois fleshed out these ideas further in *Black Reconstruction in America* (1935), where he addressed the 1930s economic, political, and cultural situation of African Americans through an examination of the Reconstruction period. Certainly the Depression was primarily what Du Bois had in mind while writing *Black Reconstruction*, but it was not the only thing. Du Bois' work with other Black intellectuals such as Carter G. Woodson (the "Father of Black History"), Alain Locke (a founder of the New Negro movement), and James Weldon Johnson (poet and author of "Lift Every Voice and Sing") during the Harlem Renaissance/New Negro movement gave his book an intellectual context.

Part of what Du Bois' *Black Reconstruction* was about was taking the Harlem Renaissance/New Negro movement beyond literature and the arts to scholarship that concentrated on the Black experience and Black contributions to American society. More than anything else, however, Du Bois' *Black Reconstruction* provided him a platform for revising the contemporary mythology given to the Reconstruction period by applying the ideas he had developed in *Souls of Black Folk* and in his 1930 Howard speech. The "Great Myth of Reconstruction"—developed by White historians and led by William Dunning at Columbia University in the early-twentieth century—was the argument that the period after the Civil War was a "tragic era," especially for ex-slaveowners and poor Whites. Northern carpetbaggers and Black freedmen were both to blame for twelve years of military occupation in the South, for White violence against Blacks, and for the rise of White supremacy in general. These scholars also blamed African Americans for their own illiteracy and poverty, and contended that corrupt Black politicians had raped both Southern White women and state treasuries. White southerners, meanwhile, did their best to create a New, more perfect, South despite these tragic obstacles.

Reconstruction from this perspective was a horrible time to be a White man from the South, rather than a period of Black faith in freedom and Black fear of terror and violence. Historians like Dunning and his students are akin to the historians, sociologists, and political scientists who have evaluated President Lyndon Johnson's Great Society/War on Poverty programs over the past thirty years. Like those Johnson administration programs, Reconstruction was a misguided attempt by liberal or "radical" politicians to change things they could not understand, as well as a ridiculous effort to help those who did not deserve it (in both cases, African Americans).

Black Reconstruction was Du Bois' way to discredit this mythical history of making heroes out of villains and victims into criminals. He wanted America to know how important African Americans were to the rebuilding of the South, and how fundamental Blacks were to the reconstruction of the White piece of the American tapestry. Du Bois was linking the truth of significant Black activism in establishing public schools and broadening state constitutions to their role as "Africans" and "Americans." Part of this role was serving as a lightning rod for the truth, the truth of Black-White relations, the truth of Black existence in America, and the truth that without "Africans," there would not be an America as we know it, not in 1935, and not in 2000. Without the "African" in America, there would not have been a need to expand democracy to include White male farmers, then all White males, and then women. Nor would there have been an Industrial Revolution of the scope that it took in America; Black sweat on the land during and after slavery turned into White dollars for rapid industrialization. Du Bois saw this as the truth of the Reconstruction period for Black and White in America, and anything else as an entertaining lie. Du Bois put it this way: "if we are going to use history for our pleasure and amusement, for inflating our national ego, and giving us a false but pleasurable sense of accomplishment," then we must "admit frankly that we are using a version of historic fact in order to…educate the new generation…the way we wish." Not only did Du Bois suggest that African Americans needed to correct history in order to provide the true story, it is also related to today's arguments on history, culture, and multicultur-alism, particularly in the History Standards debate of the 1990s. Fundamentally, the so-called "culture wars" of the past generation have been about preserving America's current truths about its history against a growing tide of history from a more human perspective. Not unlike the kind of tide Du Bois swam into in unearthing the real story of Reconstruction.

For Du Bois, *Black Reconstruction* was as much about Blacks reconstructing the White (Northern and Southern) psyche after the Civil War as it was about Africans making themselves American through their physical, cultural, legal, and intellectual reconstruction of the South and America. What did Du Bois mean when he wrote in *Black Reconstruction* that there are "physical and psychological wages of Whiteness?" That without African Americans, Whites would have so lit-tle cultural and political common ground that America would no longer exist as a country or idea. For better or worse, Du Bois saw the multiculturalism of Amer-ica tied up in the struggle of African Americans for freedom and survival, while giving Whites the ability to expand their freedoms (including the freedom to dis-crimination) at the expense of Blacks.

Du Bois was surely a multiculturalist, with a focus on the African American experience and psyche, Black-White relations, and African American advance-ment in American society. But by the time of *Black Reconstruction*, he was an increasingly dissatisfied one, and the post-World War II Communist scare did not help matters. Du Bois was forced to meet with Senator Joseph McCarthy and his sanctioned team of inquisitors in 1951, who indicted him as an unregistered agent for a foreign power because of his pro-Russian sympathies. Although Du Bois was acquitted of these charges, the House Un-American Activities Commit-tee suspended his passport and censored him for his intellectual affiliation with Marxist philosophy. Du Bois regained his passport in 1958, and after joining the Communist Party, he left the United States in 1961 for Africa and the newly independent Ghana, ruled by the Marxist President Kwame Nkrumah. In Ghana, Du Bois renounced his American citizenship and lived out the last two years of his life working on his third autobiography and an encyclopedia of Afri-can/African American history.

The dreaded term "Afrocentricity" (at least dreaded by conservatives and Whites fearful of the Africanization of America) was coined by Du Bois while working on his encyclopedia project. But this does not mean that Du Bois at age 95 had decided that his previous seven decades' worth of intellectual investments was completely worthless in his last days. One certainly could argue that Du Bois was an Afrocentrist, but only if one can show a direct link between, Du Bois,

Garvey, and Afrocentrists today. And no, Du Bois' work in Pan-Africanism during the 1920s would not be a direct link, primarily because of the movement's political, rather than cultural, makeup. If Du Bois had lived until he was 100 or 105, maybe one could fully answer this question. Because of his death in 1963, there probably will not be a full answer to this question. Du Bois' scholarship between 1903 and 1935, however, should speak for itself and for him.

Carter G. Woodson:

Carter G. Woodson also discussed Black education and the conditions African Americans faced during the Depression, as he attempted to outline a definitive educational strategy for race advancement. Like Du Bois, Woodson was disenchanted with the unwillingness of Whites to give him the recognition he deserved as a leading *American* historian. Woodson, however, held White scholars and philanthropists in contempt long before his death in 1950.

Of course, Woodson did not start this way. Born in 1875 to working-poor freedmen in rural Virginia, Woodson took a nontraditional route in making himself a trailblazing scholar. During his adolescent and early adulthood years, Woodson worked several jobs in the coal mines of West Virginia in order to support himself and his family. Woodson did not begin high school until 1895, and proceeded to complete his diploma at the Douglass High School in Huntington, West Virginia in only two years. From there, Woodson attended Berea College in Kentucky between 1897 and 1903, where he completed a bachelor's in liberal arts while serving as a school teacher at his old high school.

After four years as a federal government employee in the Philippines, Woodson decided to further his education at the University of Chicago, completing a bachelor's degree in history and a master's in Romance languages and literature in one year (1907–1908). With his first contact and advice from Du Bois in 1908, Woodson attended Harvard University, where he finished his Ph.D. in history in 1912. After some extremely negative experiences with his first thesis advisor in Edward Channing—who firmly believed in the racial inferiority of all Blacks—Woodson chose another advisor in Albert Hart (also Du Bois' advisor in the 1890s). Woodson found, however, that Hart's views of African Americans were only marginally more positive than Channing's, and struggled with the advisor over the significance of Blacks in America in the three years (1909–1912) he worked with him. By the time Woodson had completed his doctoral thesis, he had formed the opinion that White scholars found nothing of importance in studying American history from a Black perspective.

In 1912 Woodson was already 37 years old, had traveled the world, worked as a coal miner and a school teacher, and had not liked much of what he had seen of White scholarship and Whites in authority. No wonder Woodson was ready to become—as historian August Meier described Woodson—an entrepreneur for Black history. By 1915, Woodson had established the Association for the Study of Negro Life and History (ASNLH; now known as the Association for the Study of African American Life and History [ASALH]) and its corresponding *Journal of Negro History*. Woodson also published his first book in 1915, *The Education of the Negro Prior to 1861*.

In the next seven years, Woodson spent much of his time encouraging other Black intellectuals and activists such as Du Bois and Mary Church Terrell to contribute articles to his journal and seeking funds from White philanthropists for the ASNLH. When Woodson experienced difficulties publishing his books, he established Associated Publishers in 1922. Four years later, Woodson encouraged Black K-12 schools to adopt the concept of celebrating African Americans contributions to American society between George Washington's and Abraham Lincoln's birthdays in February. The segregated D.C. Public Schools was the first to implement Woodson's Negro History Week, with other schools to follow during the late-1920s and 1930s.

Woodson's projects placed him in constant contact with White scholars and philanthropists during the 1910s and 1920s. These relationships, for the most part, pushed Woodson further away from relying on White funds for projects involving the study of Black history. One would assume that Woodson is a direct philosophical ancestor of Afrocentricity. This assumption would be an oversimplification of Woodson's views of Black nationalism and Black-White relations. Woodson's experiences with White scholars, educators, and philanthropists throughout his adult life led him to believe that Whites did not want to understand African Americans or African American history. Their positions in society gave them the ability to brainwash themselves and other Americans (including Blacks) about the inferiority of Black people, African American culture, and Black contributions to American society in comparison to Whites. Woodson thought that it was his duty to research and write about what most White scholars would either ignore or lie about—the Black experience. Woodson might well be a intellectual ancestor of Afrocentricity and Black nationalism, but only in his conviction that African Americans needed a record and an understanding of their own history. This is a far different argument than the Afrocentric one, that African Americans only need to record and understand their experience and the experiences of their ancestors on the mother continent. Although Woodson might

have developed ideas that are a part of Afrocentricity today, his training, background, and work with White scholars in Black history would say otherwise.

So when Du Bois (who also served as the editor of *Crisis* magazine, the
mouthpiece of the NAACP, from 1910 to 1934) asked Woodson to give his
opinion of African American education and Black history in 1931, he saw it as
his opportunity to begin formulating a new race-empowering strategy. Considering Du Bois' Howard speech on African American educational philosophies and
Woodson's entrepreneurial work in African American history, it should not be
too surprising that Du Bois would ask Woodson to write an article on this topic.
Woodson addressed what he considered the heart of the Black education problem, the insufficient thought given by African American elites and educators to
the "needs of the people to be thus served." Woodson argued there was the need
in all of American education for teachers regardless of race to see themselves as
intellectual collaborators with the students they instruct, instead of as professionals collecting a paycheck to babysit mentally-deficient vessels. Woodson also contended that Black and White teachers should possess an understanding of and
sympathy toward Black and White culture to teach African Americans and White
students.

Woodson's article served as the foundation for his masterpiece *The Mis-education of the Negro* (1933), as he concluded that "Negro institutions of learning and
those of Whites, too…should reconstruct their curricula" to incorporate "the history and culture of the White man…and the White man should likewise learn
the same about the Negro." After nearly 40 years as both student and teacher,
Woodson realized that Blacks learning the African American experience and
Whites learning the White American experience would not help African Americans in their dealings with Whites.

Woodson's completion of his *Mis-education of the Education* brought together
his experiences as an educator, student, historian, and entrepreneur. Although
Woodson had published sixteen books before *Mis-education of the Education*—including *The Education of the Negro Prior to 1861* (1915)—this was his
first attempt to pull all of his ideas together about the direction he believed African Americans should take in their struggles for advancement. No segment of
African or mainstream America was spared in his critique, and at 58, Woodson
probably did not want to leave any doubt about his views of the Black experience
and Black education.

The Depression only added fuel to Woodson's fiery academic rhetoric that
depending on White scholars, educators, and philanthropists alone would provide African Americans a marginal position in research, limited preparation for a

White-dominated world, and few funds for Black advancement at best. At worst—which Woodson believed the case to be in 1933—White scholars would either ignore or condemn the Black experience, White educators would assume that Black students were too feeble-minded for American society, and White philanthropists would only fund projects they deemed safe regarding African Americans. Because of these circumstances, according to Woodson, "no systematic effort toward change has been possible, for, taught the same economics, history, philosophy, literature and religion...the Negro's mind has been brought under the control of his oppressor" since 1900. Woodson insisted that they could trace the cause of these circumstances to American education, a system designed to celebrate the greatness of Anglo-Saxon history and built to disregard the significance of the African American experience to America's development.

Woodson's statement in *Mis-education of the Negro* is amazingly similar to Du Bois' ideas in his Howard speech and in what Du Bois would write in *Black Reconstruction* two years later. Like Du Bois, Woodson saw a clear connection between economic discrimination, educational oppression and the role that perceived Black inferiority played in both. This belief in African American inferiority crossed racial lines, as Woodson suggested that both Blacks and Whites have been drinking from the same poisoned well of racism and fear. The fear, in this case, was of the belief in African American inferiority being proven incorrect through education, one that would celebrate the African in the American experience rather than disparage or ignore it. This fear of the "truth" also controlled the oppressor, in that believing in anything other than Black inferiority and the goodness of American education meant recognizing that Whites were responsible for creating inadequate education for African Americans. It meant acknowledging the achievements of Africans in America, and in the process, diminishing the greatness of Anglo-American accomplishments.

Much of Woodson's focus and critique in *Mis-education of the Negro* was on African American teachers. As Woodson saw it, the Black teacher had been brainwashed by the early-twentieth century system of American education

> Taught from books of the same bias, trained by Caucasians of the same prejudices or by Negroes of enslaved minds, one generation of Negro teachers after another have served no higher purpose than to do what they are told to do.

Woodson, in a very curious way, was constructing an argument about American education that White scholars would make in the 1960s and 1970s; that American education was a system designed to reproduce social classes and inequalities. The way educators and politicians designed American education, middle class students would receive a middle class education, poor students would endure a poor education, and inferior Blacks would suffer an inferior education. Although many today still see American education as American society's great equalizer, Woodson realized seven decades earlier that Americans (especially African Americans) had been "mis-educated" into this belief. As a result, "mis-educated" Black teachers and professors reproduced the conviction in African American inferiority among African American students through the application of their own "mis-education," which they received from other Black and White educators.

Woodson concluded that the Black elite, Black teachers, and Black students needed to engage each other in a quest to understand the African American experience. This quest would be comprehensive, involving a recognition of African cultural remnants in American society, a study of the history of Africans in America before the Civil War, and an acknowledgment of both the African and American essences among African Americans. Woodson wanted not only for African Americans to see the significance of his work, he also wanted all Blacks to become students of their own history in the broadest sense. Without this element, the Black elite and African American educators could continue to "mis-educate" African Americans. Woodson was doing more than arguing for an end to the Black elite as he understood it in 1933; he was demanding that ordinary Blacks take up what was considered an intellectual pursuit to achieve cultural and psychological survival. This survival would guarantee an end to Black perceptions of inferiority, and prepare African Americans for cultural, economic, and political success.

But full success would only come with the recognition of the *American* side of the African American experience. Rather than recommending the examination of the Black experience to the exclusion of the American one, Woodson suggested that Blacks study "also the history of races and nations which have been purposely ignored." African Americans should become educated "in advanced work on Shakespeare, Chaucer, and Anglo-Saxon" *and* in "the folklore of the African...[and] the works of Negro writers." By putting the African American experience on an equal footing with the Anglo-dominated version of the American experience, Woodson concluded that Blacks would push for cultural, economic, and political advancement as a result of this enlightenment. This would force Whites to confront their own beliefs about Black inferiority. It would also force the Black elite to give up their own ideas of superiority in comparison to everyday African Americans.

Woodson, in essence, possessed faith in the ability of the truth of the African American experience to transform African Americans and American society. It would enable both Blacks and Whites to recognize their multiculturally-connected history and existence. Woodson saw this period as the time to shine the light of cultural pluralism on the darkness of White supremacy and its costs to both Blacks and Whites. This light would drive out the darkness, and enable the true education of African Americans—and American society—to begin. Although Woodson's ideas from *Mis-education of the Negro* could be interpreted as representing Black nationalism or Afrocentricity, they fit almost point-by-point with Du Bois' notions as described in the Howard speech and in *Black Reconstruction.*

The immediate impact of Woodson's work went beyond a couple of book reviews and involved the ASNLH's annual meeting in the fall of 1933. The 1933 ASNLH meeting in Washington, DC and the issue of the *Journal of Negro History* (JNH) that followed in January 1934 focused on the very questions Woodson raised in *Mis-education of the Negro.* Lincoln Temple Church allowed Woodson and his ASNLH to use their building for their opening session on October 29, 1933, where a special symposium was dedicated to discussing the future of African American education. In the *Washington Tribune*, it was noted that "the auditorium of the church was packed" for these presentations. A number of presentations and the resulting essays focused on describing problems in Black education, and offered solutions that involved the introduction of the African American experience into public schools and African American colleges and universities. These essays not only echoed Woodson's call for a "re-educating of the Negro," but also served as additional evidence of multicultural Black intellectual thought on problems in African American education. The papers presented in October-November 1933 appeared as articles in a special issue of the *JNH* the following January. Much of the meeting and the articles focused on developing a curriculum that would mesh the Black experience with mainstream conceptions of American culture in all of American education.

Joseph J. Rhoads (president of Black Bishop College in Texas) argued in his article "Teaching the Negro Child" that the African American experience could help preserve and improve "the best there is in our racial character," and equalize the ranking of Blacks in the American social order. Arthur Wright (with the John F. Slater Fund) wrote in his piece "What We Should Teach the Negro Child" that an emphasis be placed on both the negative and positive aspects of the Black experience (especially economic, social, and cultural issues). Both authors realized that since race was socially constructed, culture too was constructed by those who participated in it. Rhoads and Wright contended that African Americans could reconceptualize their views and uses of their culture for educational (as opposed to entertainment) purposes.

Other writers for this issue also placed emphasis on the importance of the "contributions of each race to civilization," but with some attempts to apply this theme to contemporary trends. Herman Dreer, a Black history teacher from Sumner High School in St. Louis, composed an article in which his major concern was the effect of the Great Depression on the psyche of African Americans. Dreer implied that educating African Americans about themselves would minimize the Depression's impact on African Americans. These effects would include the "displacement of the Negro in skilled and unskilled labor...the forcing of the Negro to depend increasingly upon charity for his daily bread...and his being swept away by tuberculosis, that dread disease of poverty." Similarly, Howard University history and English professor Benjamin Brawley highlighted African America's general restlessness and rising sense of freedom that had been gained since World War I. This sense of freedom included the ability to tell the stories "of all struggles, of our aspiration and yearning, of our most earnest striving." Like Rhodes and Wright, Dreer and Brawley proposed the idea that the Black experience was a key component of educating African Americans to survive and overcome their circumstances.

It was clear to these educators that a mostly segregated education about the achievements of Anglo and other White Americans had not inspired Blacks as a group to high achievement in education or in any other arena. The previous decade and a half of significant Black migration, the cultural revolutions of the Harlem Renaissance and the New Negro movement, and even the messianic nationalism of Marcus Garvey's UNIA program all pointed in the direction of educating Blacks about themselves. These authors believed that a more accurate picture of African American struggles and triumphs, when presented in a formal educational context, would embolden Blacks to survive despite the Depression and achieve despite discrimination and violence.

With the Depression and his struggles to obtain funds from the White foundation community, Woodson became more persistent and overbearing on the issue of funding for the ASNLH. Woodson only wanted to work on ASNLH research projects that received their funding from Blacks, and desired for Blacks from all walks of life to become involved with the organization. In 1936, Woodson complained to the *Washington Afro-American* about the Phelps-Stokes Fund's effort to publish an "encyclopedia of the Negro" through a combined authorship of Du Bois and an unnamed White author.

Woodson contended that it was ludicrous to allow a research project on the African/African American experience to receive funding from Whites who have believed in Black inferiority and White superiority for three centuries. Du Bois, according to Woodson, should have embarked on this project without White money or White intellectual collaboration. Woodson declared that any "man who carries out a project led by Anson Phelps Stokes and Thomas Jesse Jones, to put in permanent form what they and their co-workers think of the colored, is a traitor to his race." Woodson had been offered co-editorialship of the encyclopedia by the Phelps-Stokes Fund at $8,000, but turned it down, citing previous attempts of the Fund to control the direction of his research. One must also consider Woodson's growing frustrations with the consistent rejection he had received since the beginning of the Depression from the foundation world for his projects. The Phelps-Stokes encyclopedia project, in any case, never fully moved forward, and had only produced one volume by the time the project died in 1945.

For the decade and a half between *Mis-education of the Negro* and his death in April 1950, Woodson continued in his groundbreaking research on African American history, but without the financial support he had garnered during the 1910s and 1920s. In spite of this, Woodson produced research and ideas that powerfully influenced the development of African American history, Black Studies, and Afrocentricity. But Woodson's work also contributed to the development of multicultural ideas among African Americans, specifically in the context of education.

Alain L. Locke:

The twentieth-century Black philosopher Alain Locke had intellectual relationships with Du Bois and Woodson, and yet produced a truly unique body of work on multiculturalism. Locke, was more familiar with multiculturalism than either Du Bois or Woodson. Born in 1886 to school-teaching parents in Philadelphia, Locke's excellent school work enabled him to attend Harvard in 1904. He completed his bachelor's degree in philosophy in three years, and became the first African American Rhodes Scholar in 1907. After three years at Oxford and a year at the University of Berlin (where he finished a bachelor's in literature), Locke returned to the U.S. in 1912 to teach at Howard University. While at Howard, Locke enrolled at Harvard again (in 1916), this time for a doctorate in philosophy, which he completed in 1918.

What makes this narrative version of Locke's educational career interesting besides the obvious high level of achievement is who Locke worked with while at

Harvard. His professors and instructors included philosophers William James, George Santayana, and Horace Kallen. Like Du Bois, Locke worked with one of the founding fathers of American philosophy and psychology in William James as an undergraduate at Harvard, and kept in contact with the intellectual until James' death in 1910. Locke also studied under philosopher George Santayana in both his undergraduate and doctoral years. One of the single most important Harvard contacts in Locke's studies and scholarship, however, was Horace Kallen, who was the first instructor to directly introduce Locke to multicultural-ism's parallel term cultural pluralism. Locke picked up the term firsthand as it originated from a class at Harvard taught by then teacher assistant Horace Kallen in 1906. This made Locke one of the first intellectuals Black, White, or otherwise to encounter and use this idea. While Du Bois certainly was exposed to pluralist philosophy during his undergraduate days at Harvard, Du Bois did not deliber-ately develop an intellectual agenda (particularly pursuing a Ph.D. in philosophy) around this topic. This of course was what Locke had done in his career. Besides being a key instructor in Locke's pre-Rhodes Scholar studies, Kallen and Locke became friends when both were at Oxford between 1907 and 1910, worked on a number of different writing projects together, and remained friends until Locke's death in 1954.

Kallen and Locke had similar careers when it came to defining and using the term cultural pluralism. Sociologist Rutledge M. Dennis stressed that just as Kallen was interested in cultural pluralism specifically in terms of the Jewish iden-tity, Locke focused specifically on the African American experience. Dennis noted that both Kallen and Locke "sought to demythologize and demystify the idea of democracy as only implying a majority role in which minorities would be voiceless." In an essay dedicated to Alain Locke in 1955, Kallen himself wrote that they both believed in "this endeavor toward friendship by people who are so different from each other but who, as different, hold themselves equal to each other."

Although Locke and Kallen only examined the relationship between American democracy, pluralism, and their respective ethnic groups, that did not mean that Locke was Afrocentric nor that Kallen was Jewish-centered. Putting African Americans and the African American experience on an equal footing with the dominant American culture was Locke's ultimate goal, not the separation of Afri-can Americans from American society, nor the extinction of the "African" in the African American experience. Similarly, Kallen's foremost goal was to place Jew-ish culture on an equal cultural plain with Anglo-American culture. Du Bois, Woodson, Locke, and Kallen all ultimately saw American culture as one dominated by White Anglo-Saxon Protestant ideals, and all four believed that the inclusion and recognition of non-WASP cultural contributions to the American fabric was necessary if America was ever going to live up to its creed.

In the spring of 1916, Locke gave a series of lectures at Howard University on "Race Contacts and Interracial Relations." Jeffrey Stewart—the editor of Locke's lectures—noted that the blatant imperialism that Locke saw as the cause of World War I, and his discussions of cultural pluralism with Kallen, Du Bois, and Miller facilitated what Locke later called the "Great Disillusionment." This transformation led directly to the Howard lectures in 1916, and probably to Locke's attendance at Harvard for his doctorate. Disillusionment for Locke was apparently a wonderful experience, for it sparked him to address issues of race, culture, and civilization in a way he had not considered before, and it put him on his own path of cultural pluralism.

In the lecture "Racial Progress and Adjustment," Locke suggested that American society's poor attempts to assimilate African Americans had also been limited by Blacks themselves. This was because African Americans had been denied the ability to possess long-standing ethnic traditions by slavery, which had resulted in the discarding of any traditions by many Blacks (particularly the elite) that even seemed "African" in essence. Locke contended that of the next generation of African American intellectuals must work to salvage everything of value that links the Black experience to its African past. Locke concluded that "the goal of race progress and race adjustment" was the promotion of "culture-citizenship," which "must come in terms of group contribution to what becomes a joint civilization."

Locke argued that because White Americans really did not have to partake of the traditions of other cultures, they had created a process in which other groups (including African Americans) would have to adopt at least some Western values in order to survive. Vestiges of the "African" in African American culture, despite slavery and discrimination, remained a part of the Black experience as "tradition" into the early twentieth century. Future African American cultural development depended upon both the assimilation of White American culture and the recognition of African "traditions" within the African American experience. Locke's argument was for a multicultural society, one which recognized the different cultures that existed within its borders while also accepting that all of these groups possess the rights of all citizens—to live, vote, and prosper. This was what Locke meant by "culture-citizenship," that all Americans—including African Americans—had the right to maintain their diversity while becoming active participants in a larger society with differing sets of values. Although David Levering Lewis described Locke as a fan of assimilation during the Harlem Renaissance period in his *When Harlem Was in Vogue* (1982), Locke would not argue for integration without maintaining that Blacks needed to preserve their African heritage and the African American experience. By definition, Locke would be an advocate of multiculturalism rather than assimilation or Afrocentricity.

Locke's work during the 1920s and 1930s also depicted a strategy of multiculturalism that would take advantage of the best that the Black experience offered without downplaying the connections between American culture and the Black community. The appearance of Locke's edited volume *The New Negro* in 1925 was evidence of the Black community's impact upon its intellectuals, as many up-and-coming members of the African American intelligentsia were from the Black working-class. In the introduction that bears the book's title, Locke contended that since the start of the First World War there had been major changes in the lifestyles of African Americans. While a large physical transformation was occurring because of the migration of hundreds of thousands of Blacks from the rural South to the urban Northeast and Midwest, another transformation beyond demographics was taking place in Black thought. This revolution of thought was the key to understanding the rise of the "New Negro," those African Americans who were proud of their heritage and proud of their contributions to American society. Locke also determined that should these "New Negroes" pass down their newfound knowledge and freedom of thought to succeeding generations, it would pave the way for Black empowerment and advancement.

In explaining the rise of the "New Negro" irrespective of social class, Locke wrote that "all classes of a people under social pressure are permeated with a common experience; they are emotionally welded as others cannot be." One can easily conclude from this statement that Locke argued that a community of collective experience was what made African Americans who they were. If this is all one takes from Locke's statement, then one could make the argument that Locke was a friend of Black nationalism, which was definitely not the case. One could assume instead that Locke's emphasis here was on the common experience of African Americans for two related reasons. The first was that the New Negro movement and the Great Migration that led to it had proved bothersome to the "Old Negroes" or the old Black elite, who were committed to assimilation *minus* the celebration of the Black experience. In conjunction with this revelation was the reality that the New Negro movement and the Harlem Renaissance reflected a much wider diversity of thought among African Americans than Whites or the Black elite were willing to admit.

According to historian Mia Bay in her *The White Image in the Black Mind* (2000), Locke was also responding to the relatively new idea that race was constructed by groups and societies rather than determined by biology or geography. Locke's way of distancing himself from the biological uniqueness of African Americans was to underscore that the "social pressures" of slavery's legacy, systematic discrimination, and economic exploitation combined to give African Americans a common cultural experience, even in the midst of their diversity. Although this could indicate the shift that Bay discussed in her study, it also reveals Locke's recognition of culture in the American and Black contexts as both constructed and fluid, which would explain both commonalities and differences within African America. Locke's statement should be examined for what it implies as much as for what it says, in that Locke's declaration of a common Black experience indirectly acknowledged the diversity within the Black community. In recognizing the common bonds between Blacks, Locke was also illuminating the multicultural essence of African Americans, a theme that he would explore further during the 1930s and 1940s.

An examination of Locke's work during the 1920s often gives one the impression that Locke was in the midst of an intellectual balancing act between the promotion of the African American experience and the realization that the Black experience is inseparably linked to the mainstream American experience. Nothing indicates this more than Locke's work to promote African/African American history, culture, and art to both Blacks and Whites. Locke called for Whites to accept African notions of art and beauty in *The New Negro* and in numerous articles throughout his career. At the same time, Locke pressed for an African Studies department at Howard University between 1928 and 1938, taking up sociology professor Kelly Miller's cause. Miller had also pushed Howard to create an African Studies department in 1909 and 1915, but the university's predominantly White administrators rejected his proposals.

In 1926, theologian Mordecai Johnson had become the first African American president of Howard, and was considered to be someone who would push hard for a strong curriculum related to the Black experience by the university's Black faculty. In June 1928, Locke sent a memo to Johnson that contained an outline for an African Studies department. Locke reasoned that the primary purpose of a Black university was to be a "center for the research study of the problems of Negro group life" and a "center of counsel and guidance for intelligent group action." Locke included courses in African/African American history, cultural anthropology, education, and African art and culture in his memo to Johnson. Johnson thought the idea for an African Studies department a good one, but would not act on it for a decade. The Depression's negative impact on Howard's cash flow would keep Johnson from establishing an African Studies department until Locke and Miller fought for it again in 1938. What became known as the Moorland-Spingarn Research Center for the collection of African and African American history and culture was created as a result of the efforts of Locke and Miller. Howard would not establish an African Studies department until 1953, and an Afro-American Studies department until 1969.

By 1935, Locke's attempts to popularize African American history and culture led him to address the rise of the intercultural education movement among a group of liberal White scholars throughout the urban Northeast, particularly at Columbia University's Teachers College and New York University in New York. Intercultural education is a cousin of multiculturalism because of its emphasis on the tolerance of White ethnic groups, but it is not much more than that because of its limited work on tolerance towards people of color. Locke composed the essay "Minorities and the Social Mind" for the intercultural education-affiliated journal *Progressive Education* in March 1935. In it, he argued that the cultures of many non-dominant groups in Anglo-dominated American society continued to exist, albeit under difficult circumstances. For Locke, the typical mainstream American assumption that ignoring cultural, racial, and religious differences would allow these variations to wither on the vine of conformity ran counter to the racist activism of assimilation and violence against diversity and its bearers. This remains an assumption that most Americans hold to today, to the impairment of our society.

Education was the key to solving such problems of diversity—and to eliminating the tensions of this dilemma between cultural indifference and culture wars—particularly among mainstream Whites. Locke recommended an educational approach that placed children "in sample social experiences with the life and folk-ways of minority groups" with a "more formal intellectual acquaintance with the historical and cultural reasons for these interesting differences." Locke believed that the circle of cultural pluralism within America's schools would only be completed with everyday physical contact between mainstream students and students of almost every conceivable cultural, racial, and religious background.

This essay is more than a combining of multiculturalism and desegregation as strategies. Locke would have seen multiculturalism and desegregation as part of the same process for Black advancement, White acknowledgment, and American ascendance beyond cultural and racial strife. "Minorities and the Social Mind" also revealed Locke's understanding of ethnicity and race beyond Black and White, specifically that "Whites" were not a singular group. Rather, Locke recognized that "Whites" really referenced a variety of groups united by ideas of racial difference and superiority when compared to African Americans, separate when compared to each other. While these distinctions among White Americans are not as relevant today (thanks in part to the intercultural education movement), they still exist in large measure.

It was Locke's idea that these variations should not be eradicated, but exploited in a positive manner, as a strength of American society and for all groups within it. This line of thought lines up squarely with Du Bois' ideas from *Souls of Black Folk*, except that Locke held *all* groups (including African Americans) would benefit from an examination of their own and one another's essences. This is the fundamental criteria of multiculturalism, and is also why Locke called for both cultural and demographic/physical integration of K-12 schools. Locke continued his work in cultural pluralism with both Black and White scholars through the 1940s, and passed away in 1954 having made a significant impact on both African American and White thought on multiculturalism.

African American Women Intellectuals, Multiculturalism, and Desegregation:

Writings by Black women around issues of race relations, culture, and race uplift contained the third dimension of gender in addition to race and class. A *multicultural* examination for Black women involves their African-ness, American-ness, and womanhood along with their consideration of Anglo-American women and culture. African American women intellectuals, scholars, and educators firmly believed that Black women had to play a significant role in the elevation of Blacks if they were to advance at all. This belief did not match the views of White women who were merely seeking to improve their own lot.

As African American women's historian Elsa Barkley Brown has indicated, the racial and gender consciousness of Black women is more fully described by the term "womanism" than by feminism. Building on the work of writer-activist Alice Walker and professor-activist Chikwenye Okonjo Ogunyemi, Brown defined womanism as a consciousness that "incorporates racial, cultural, sexual, national, economic, and political considerations." Feminism and the Feminist movement—as noted by Brown, Walker, Ogunyemi, Darlene Clark Hine, Paula Giddings, Kimberle Crenshaw, bell hooks, and Patricia Hill Collins (among many others)—had neglected issues of race and culture in promoting the equal rights of *White* woman. At the same time, movements like Black nationalism and Afrocentricity had proven unable to fully incorporate issues of women's rights because of the dominance of African American men who were only concerned with race. According to multicultural theorist Gloria Ladson-Billings, the concept of womanism gives African American women and other women of color a vehicle for challenging racial, gender, and class oppression. This realization fits in well with multiculturalism, in that womanism has allowed African American women to reflect on who they are based on their own, White women's, and Black men's perceptions.

Anna J. Cooper:

Perhaps no one embodied notions of womanism at the beginning of the twentieth century more than Anna Julia Cooper. Cooper's lifespan bridges the gap between the Supreme Court's *Dred Scott* decision of 1857 (she was probably born in 1858), which declared that the Black man possessed no rights that the White man was bound to respect, and the Civil Rights Act of 1964. Cooper was the daughter of slave Hannah Stanley and her White master, and grew up with her mother in Raleigh, North Carolina during and after Emancipation. The Renaissance woman began her formal education in 1867 at the Episcopal Church's St. Augustine's Normal and Collegiate Institute in Raleigh, where she received training to become a teacher. In 1877, she married her namesake George A. C. Cooper, a Black Episcopal priest who died two years later. This was obviously a life-changing event for Cooper, who never re-married. She instead finished her training to become a teacher and then enrolled at Oberlin College in Ohio in 1881, where she first met future educator and activist Mary Church (soon to be Mary Church Terrell). Cooper completed her bachelor's in 1884, and earned a master's in teacher training from Oberlin while teaching at Wilberforce in Ohio and St. Augustine's.

Moving to Washington, DC after finishing her master's, Cooper took a position at the recently established M Street High School, the bastion of elite Black public school education throughout the segregation era. Cooper would remain a fixture there as a teacher and principal (with the exception of the years 1906 to 1911) until 1930, when she was forced into retirement. Five years earlier, Cooper became the fourth African American woman to earn a doctorate at the Sorbonne in Paris; her thesis was French attitudes toward slavery during the French Revolutionary period.

Why do we not know more about the life and achievements of Anna Julia Cooper? Because she was an intellectual Black woman in an era dominated by men (mostly White), and because Cooper never deliberated aligned herself with powerful allies such as Booker T. Washington. Cooper's unique talents and lack of social status made her an anomaly within the Black elite, and added to the obscurity she would have experienced anyway as an African American woman in a White-dominated society.

Cooper developed ideas that we would now consider a part of womanism and multiculturalism today. Her ideas paralleled and preceded Du Bois' regarding the Black experience serving as a vehicle for race advancement, but with a gendered dimension. In Cooper's classic *A Voice from the South* (1892), she pulled race, gender, class, and culture together to address the so-called race question and where Black women should locate themselves in that question. Realizing the special position of African American women on issues of race and gender, Cooper also recognized that this uniqueness meant Black women had two strikes against them in their race work. Cooper claimed that African American women had little support from Whites and even less encouragement from Black men. As Cooper put it, "the colored woman too often finds herself hampered and shamed by a less liberal sentiment and a more conservative attitude on the part of those for whose opinion she cares most." So Cooper understood that the Black woman's unique position in American society would give her the ability to provide new ideas and different strategies for African American social, cultural, political, and economic advancement and for American society's benefit. She argued that without contributions from African American women, the Black community would not survive, and American society would surely decline.

To be sure, Cooper saw the fusion between race and gender that Black women personified as *the* key to the success of African Americans. Cooper viewed the African American experience as relatively undeveloped, and saw an opportunity for Black women to play a leading role in the construction of their people's experience. Cooper believed that "to be a woman of the Negro race in America, and to be able to grasp the deep significance of the possibilities of the crisis, is to have a heritage, it seems to me, unique in the ages." Cooper envisioned the "colored woman's office" as one of a cultural gatekeeper constructing and preserving the African American identity. But while Cooper felt that Black women as parents should seek to raise their sons and daughters to achieve in American society, she also realized that educated Black women (the elite) would play the most significant role in moving the race forward. Cooper's thought, while somewhat elitist, also held out hope that African American women irrespective of social class would take up the mantle of race improvement.

The major point made by Cooper was that African American women needed to comprehend themselves as African, American, and as women. Some scholars would argue that Cooper's perspective of her "womanhood" relied too heavily on White and Victorian notions of it. Even so, Cooper's aforementioned statement goes well beyond an understanding of the ideal Black woman as simply chaste, cultured, and compliant to honorable Black men. What Cooper had done was construct an argument favoring Black women's ideas for African American progress. She concluded that the strategies of sincere Whites (male and female) and Black men had hardly been enough in the quarter-century between the end of slavery and the beginning of Jim Crow to alleviate Black suffering and engender race uplift.

Cooper applied concepts of multiculturalism directly and practically to the situation of African American women. She first located Black women as culturally special because of their Black, American, and female components. Cooper examined other groups who could not embody all three categories, specifically White men, White women, and Black men. She discovered from her analysis the revelation that Black women had yet to make their unique contribution to understanding the African American experience or to Anglo-American culture. In declaring the necessity of the Black women's voice on issues of race, gender, and culture, Cooper's *Voice from the South* was her own multicultural, womanist voice, somewhat elitist and yet somewhat inclusive at the same time.

More than forty years later, Cooper wrote a short, poignant essay further demonstrating her multicultural thought. Cooper's "Equality of the Races and the Democratic Movement" (1925) combined her religious curiosity with her intellectual zeal to comment on the concept of equality and the relative lack of it in modern Western culture. In considering Western culture's need for love, mercy, justice, and humility in the presence of God, Cooper determined that the promotion and proliferation of equality was key to stem cultural decline. She wrote that it

> is not for the little fellow who swells up with the idea I am as good as the other fellow; but for the big fellow with all the power and all the controls to stop and consider: The other fellow is as good as I am. Both human, both mortal, both entitled to a place in the sun.

This essay was a response to the horrors of World War I (22 million dead), the genocide of colonialism, and White America's rejection of its non-White heritage and peoples. Cooper argued that it was not enough for people of color to acknowledge their own cultural heritage and humanity, but that Whites also had to recognize the heritage and humanity of non-Whites.

When combined with Cooper's thought of 43 years earlier, it is fairly evident that Cooper was an intellectual antecedent of multiculturalism and womanism.

Cooper might not have suggested that K-12 schools include the Black experience as part of their curriculum or considered the souls of *all* Black folks. But despite her popular culture and mainstream academic obscurity, she did lay groundwork for the development of womanism and multiculturalism at a time in which many considered Black women incapable of such a feat.

For African American intellectuals and scholars, the 1925–40 period served as a watershed for multicultural formulations. The oppressive effects of the Depression—along with the liberating impact of the Harlem Renaissance, the New Negro movement, the Garvey movement, and the Great Migration—forced the Black intelligentsia to consider multiculturalism as an alternative to the turn-of-the-century strategies of industrial and classical education. A number of Black intellectuals and educators suggested strategies that combined both multiculturalism and desegregation into one that addressed the discrimination of the larger society and the need for empowered community institutions.

But these intellectual considerations could not have occurred without the foundation of intellectual thought that had been constructed at the turn of the century. It was not a coincidence that *New Negro* and *Mis-education of the Negro* came a generation after the *Souls of Black Folk* and *Voice from the South*; the earlier ideas helped to influence the later ones. Nor was it a mere accident that the ideas that intellectuals such as Du Bois, Woodson, Locke, and Cooper continued to evolve as key changes took hold within African America, changes that confirmed many of their conclusions.

If one were to examine the ideas of scholars, educators, and intellectuals such as James Weldon Johnson, Mary McLeod Bethune, E. Franklin Frazier, Ida B. Wells, Rayford Logan, and Walter White, would one draw the same conclusions regarding the development of multicultural thought among African Americans? Although one could make the argument that Du Bois, Woodson, Locke, and Cooper are not representative of *all* Black intellectuals from this period, they represent so *many* different perspectives that it becomes unnecessary to analyze the intellectual texts of every Black intellectual in one setting. There is also the reality that more work is necessary on the interaction of Black intellectuals, particularly among African American women, around multicultural issues.

For Du Bois, Woodson, Cooper, and Locke to a large extent, the Depression and the key events that coincided with it meant that African Americans were at a crossroads. For Du Bois and Woodson in particular, the Depression was an opportunity for either assured destruction or for laying the foundation for prosperity. These scholars and intellectuals chose to view this period as one in which the best minds could contemplate the best strategies for ending legal segregation, thriving in the midst of social segregation, and growing in the process of cultural inclusion.

This story of intense intellectual outpouring is one that has been neglected by historians and other scholars. Somehow, the history reads that Black intellectual development occurred mostly in the areas of integration and Black nationalism, reached its height during the Harlem Renaissance (emphasis on "Harlem" here), underwent rapid decline in conjunction with the Stock Market Crash, and did rise again until after World War II. At the very least, White intellectuals were not the only ones who were writing about what had happened to America and its economic, social, political, and cultural prosperity after 1929. It is more important for one to recognize, however, that the headiness of African Americans during the 1920s and 1930s has been part of a circle of thought that stretched back to the end of slavery, and extends to the current crises of African America. This circle of thought did more than respond to a particular crisis, because African Americans have almost always faced a crisis of one sort or another. These were years full of ideas because so many crises and possibilities had come together at the same time and in the right proportions.

Part Two: Practicing Multiculturalism,
African American Style

3

Walking By Faith:
Multiculturalism, Identity, And
Black Washington

"I'm looking out for your best interests" was what my dissertation advisor typically said in discussing my future with me. As far as my advisor was concerned, he was in charge of the rest of my academic career, determining everything from whether I would finish my doctorate to where I would live and work after I graduated. But as I would discover by the end of my education, he was not nurturing my career at all.

Virtually all of my achievements as a graduate student occurred despite my advisor rather than because of him. This was because my advisor discouraged my attempts to publish, to obtain grants for my research, to participate in major conferences, and to apply for jobs when it was apparent I had nearly completed my doctoral thesis. My advisor would frequently say "You're not ready" to take on a particular project or to apply for a grant or job to hinder my efforts.

One of our last official meetings as advisor and student covered this particular issue. Six chapters into an eight-chapter dissertation, I was still being told that I was "not ready" to apply for jobs or to attend major conferences. My advisor had in fact contradicted some of what he had said about my work in a previous meeting. So when he declared for the eighteenth time in this particular meeting that he was not giving me his support because he was "looking out for my best interests," I sarcastically replied "Yeah, right!" I decided that I could not abide the hypocrisy of an advisor who cared little for my future while at the same time professing to care very deeply.

For any academic scholar who reads this, they will conclude that I committed academic suicide by exhibiting such defiance to my advisor. The reality is that my advisor committed a form of academic suicide by refusing to promote at least one student's career development. Besides having one's work published and obtaining grants, developing new talent is key to creating a legacy as a successful professor.

Beyond the trials and tribulations of a young intellectual, the reason this anecdote is important is because it represents in miniature what "elite" African Americans have done in their interactions with "ordinary" Blacks. Of course, a Black person working on a Ph.D. is far from ordinary in most people's eyes, but facing the patronizing opposition of powerful people while finishing the degree (or in doing anything else) *is* a typical description of abusive power. Black elites harnessed their social, cultural, and intellectual power to dictate how all Blacks should act in public, should think concerning racial advancement, and with whom they should privately associate. For many powerful African Americans, ordinary Blacks were "not ready" to decide these issues on their own. While alleging to act in the interests of all African Americans, hindsight shows that many in the Black elite were more concerned with raising their own status than with improving the daily lives of everyday Blacks. Certainly this is not to say that all elite Blacks were insincere in their words and work to uplift the race, but most elite African Americans suggested strategies that in the long run would benefit their worldview more than the lives of their non-elite comrades. Like my African American dissertation advisor, many in the Black elite believed *their* ideas contained the magic solution to the future of ordinary Black folk.

When historians and other scholars engage the subject of African American attempts at advancement, the same tired terms "integration" and "nationalism" are touted in their descriptions of Black protest and struggle. These terms are loaded with a century's worth of connotations, from integration meaning "assimilation" and "becoming White" to nationalism signifying "separatism," "Black pride," and "militancy." There is the unwritten assumption that we can categorize the historical struggle of African Americans for equality and progress into these two basic philosophies. What is equally important is that these divergent ideologies coincide almost exclusively with class distinctions among African Americans. "Integrationists" are typically "wanna be like White" middle class or elite Blacks, whereas "nationalists" usually are "I'm Blacker than Black" working-class or poor Blacks.

There are a set of ideas among some African American historians that the two-headed animal alleged to represent the ideologies of Black advancement is far more complex. African American historian Kevin Gaines suggests that the African American elite's embracement of a "racial uplift" philosophy during the early twentieth century inadvertently perpetuated racist stereotypes in their attempts to distance themselves from the allegedly uncivilized behavior of the Black masses.

For Gaines, the Black elite's racial uplift philosophy was a double-edged sword, with one edge dedicated to raising the status of all Blacks through elite guidance, and the other serving to sever ties between the elite and their ordinary brethren. Fellow Black cultural historian Robin D. G. Kelley argues that working-class and poor African Americans have supported many official elite Black efforts to end racial discrimination, but like any diverse group of people, they had their own nuanced and relatively "hidden" views of Black advancement. Non-elite African Americans did not automatically assume that integration would bring access to mainstream society's institutions and success for themselves and their children. Their educational attainment and class position relative to elite Blacks made it much less likely that they could assimilate.

Focusing on examples of multiculturalism among non-elite Blacks certainly falls under the category of "hidden" transcript. In exploring the Black Washington, DC community of the late-1920s and 1930s, what we are looking at would be argued by many as either examples of integrationist or nationalist philosophies. Multiculturalism is neither philosophy, but contains elements of both. Multiculturalism in everyday practice insists neither for total Black assimilation into White America nor for total Black separation from mainstream society in a physical or cultural way. As the experiences of Black Washingtonians illustrate, multiculturalism was a pragmatic means to instill the African American experience into their children and community at a time when it was excluded from the public schools. These everyday Blacks acted irrespective of Black elite views to discover for themselves what being "Black" meant, and what kind of education would best benefit their children.

At the same time, many Black Washingtonians also believed that understanding mainstream American society was paramount. This tension within the multicultural views of African Americans, which was unapparent during the 1930s, has certainly become so in the last decade of the twentieth century and in the early twenty-first, as the controversy over Afrocentricity and multiculturalism among African Americans suggests. What we are investigating is the precursor to the current debate about multiculturalism's ability to promote equality in American society and to encourage group pride.

An examination of Blacks in the Nation's Capital is important because it foreshadows many cultural, economic, and social changes that Blacks would face throughout urban America in the post-1945 period. These changes include the increasing migration of Blacks to cities, White movement to the suburbs, Black overcrowding in the public schools, and increasing insistence for desegregation.

Ultimately this is a confirmation of the "walk by faith" of working-class Blacks toward equality despite severe racial discrimination, economic hardship and exploitation, and even elite indifference. They acted out of their own best interests in learning about their history, their culture, and their community. Of course ordinary Blacks wanted to be entertained (to the chagrin of elites), but certainly some of their celebration occurred in an educational context. And although their "walk by faith" was not one which invested heavily in multiculturalism as we know it, everyday African Americans recognized that they needed to fortify themselves with the knowledge of their African and American essences in their walk through an unforgiving world. Despite the significant intraracial divide, ordinary and elite Blacks even occasionally worked together in making the multicultural self-discovery process one of action as much as one of ideas.

Intrarace Relations and Education in Black Washington, 1925–40:

Before launching into an examination of the Black Washington community's activities and how they lend themselves to understanding multiculturalism, one needs to understand the nature of this Black community and the circumstances it faced in the first third of the twentieth century. There are two reasons to give a brief description of the early-twentieth-century African American community in Washington. One is that it illustrates in many ways problems that urban Black communities throughout the United States have faced since the 1920s, from overcrowding and migration to significant class divisions and elitist proposals to address economic problems with moral solutions. The other is because one must understand whether the ideas and actions toward multiculturalism by Black Washingtonians are consistent with the conditions and circumstances that they faced in the 1920s and 1930s. Could such high-minded activities occur despite segregation, the Great Depression, and conservative elite activities that may or may not have been compatible with multiculturalism?

"Saturday Night and the Negro," for example—a 1928 article from the Black weekly newspaper *Washington Tribune*—was written to critique the extracurricular activities of "two women of the laboring classes." The author used these two non-elite Black women as examples of deviant behavior among all working-class African Americans, for they spent their Saturday nights engaged in "uneconomic buying" and "economic thriftless[ness]." According to the author, the Black church was at fault in neglecting to "direct the emotions of the race from channels which suited jungle life into channels which make for economic survival." Believing that Saturday night activities like "partying" were both detrimental to and hypocritical for Blacks to engross themselves in, the author noted in the article's last sentence that "every Saturday night comes ahead of Sunday." The hypocrisy, according to the author, was in two women involving themselves in unrighteous activities within twelve hours of attending church (assuming, of course, they did go to church).

Whoever the author was, it is a safe bet that he or she was part of Washington's African American elite. This author confirms both Gaines' and Kelley's arguments regarding how the Black elite evaluated the extracurricular activities of their non-elite counterparts; they saw them as uncivilized or "jungle." Certainly the author's comments were intended to effect changes in what s/he perceived as negative social behavior among working-class Black Washingtonians, but the comments also confirm White prejudices and perceptions of all Black activities. And as Gaines has also made clear, Black elites engaged in "economically thriftless" activities themselves, including illegal ones (at least during the 1920s and early 1930s) such as drinking at nightclubs and playing the "numbers game." In any case, non-elite Black Washingtonians created and participated in a variety of community institutions for themselves that could not be considered "jungle" by any standards, including churches, social organizations, leisure activities like movies, theater, and dance. Rank-and-file African Americans established institutions and activities independent of elite Black thought and actions.

Part of the reason for this class segregation stemmed from the reality that elites created their own exclusive institutions and activities. For elite Black Washingtonians, private fraternal organizations and clubs provided a source of entertainment and social gathering—read "showing off" here—that again set them apart from less socially-prominent African Americans. Two such organizations were the Mu-Sa-Lit Club (a.k.a., Music and Literary Social Club) and the Bethel Literary and Historical Association. Native Black Washingtonian Edward Feggans reminisced that in the social activities at the historically Black Howard University, most "of the sororities, the fraternities, and the recognized people, were light-skinned…or you were a professional's daughter or…a doctor's daughter, or a lawyer's daughter, or something like that."

District Black elites also segregated themselves from the rest of the community based on class and color in the D.C. Public Schools. Felicia Chisley (who was a student in D.C. Public Schools from 1932 to 1948 and taught there from 1948 to 1980) acknowledged that when she attended D. C. Public Schools during the 1930s, "there was no question at that time that there was a great color thing with us." She also recalled that at elite Black Dunbar High School

[t]here was indeed partiality. That's the truth of it, that there was partiality at Dunbar. Unfortunately, we frequently equate a person's worth by what their parents do...there were some things, class things, even within the school that were very prominent.

Chisley mentioned that a friend of hers from a working-class family had been denied entry into the National Honor Society at Dunbar because a couple of elite upperclassmen had applied for college admission, and needed the membership on their transcript to enhance their chances of getting accepted. Chisley concluded angrily with her belief that "indeed it was [an intraracial class and color line], and anyone who tells you it wasn't is not telling the truth or is living in a dream world or has amnesia!"

For Chisley, the Dunbar experience was obviously discriminatory towards darker-skinned Blacks and African Americans without the right parental pedigree. One has to consider that because Dunbar was the elite high school of D.C. Public Schools irrespective of color, even darker-skinned "nobodies" fared much better educationally than most African American students in the other District schools. One should also realize that for popular, elite, light-skinned Black students during the 1920s and 1930s, Dunbar was a "dream world" of possibilities, allowing those students to wax nostalgic about their wonderful years at the center of attention.

Dunbar High School by the 1920s and 1930s was a Black elite K-12 educational mecca with a national reputation for high achievement and status among African Americans. The school was originally the M Street High School, and was built in 1887 to provide the late-nineteenth century Black elite with a school for their children. Mary Church Terrell and Anna Julia Cooper had both served as principals of the M Street High School during its first two decades. By the mid-1910s, articles (including one by Terrell) were being written about the quality of the teachers and students at M Street High School, ranking it equal to the best lily-White private schools in the country. But growing enrollment meant that a new building would be needed to house the Black elite's pride and joy.

This, however, was only part of the reason the M Street High School was moved, as it did not keep its original name. Roscoe Conklin Bruce—former M Street principal and Superintendent for the Black public schools—had allowed Dutch anthropologist H. M. Bernelot Moens to conduct a so-called ethnographic study of Black schoolchildren by taking nude pictures of his subjects in 1915. Over the next three years, Moens proceeded to have sexual relations with an African American female student and a Black teacher in the midst of his "research" at M Street. After a lengthy investigation by the District in conjunction with what we now call the FBI, Moens was deported to the Netherlands. Bruce, meanwhile, would eventually lose his job, due in large measure to his incompetent handling of the whole affair, as well as because of his ties to the late Booker T. Washington. As a result of the move, the Moens debacle, and the need to celebrate a deceased Black Washingtonian, the M Street High School was renamed the Paul Lawrence Dunbar High School, named after the late but great young Black poet of the early 1900s.

Chester and Enez Martin also recounted the intraracial problems (however hidden) of D. C. Public Schools, and more specifically, Dunbar High School. Both grew up in the District during the 1920s and 1930s, with Chester Martin attending D.C. Public Schools and Dunbar, and Enez Martin enrolled from K through eighth grade (she attended a Catholic high school). Mrs. Martin argued that "within Dunbar, there was a kind of class" division between light-skinned students and those whose parents worked in professional fields and the other Dunbar students. Mr. Martin concurred, pointing out that "most of the [academically] outstanding students appeared to be people of a light complexion, except myself. I was the kind of guy who just got by by the skin of my teeth." Mr. Martin, who himself is light-skinned, evoked the response "[b]ut you see, they accepted you" from his wife, who maintained that color was more important than achievement at Dunbar. With that statement, Mr. Martin recognized that while "we had a few Blacks who were darker in color in Dunbar [who] were outstanding...for the most part, most of the outstanding Blacks were light-skinned Blacks, and their parents were in very good jobs in the government. Or else, they were sons of doctors and lawyers and professional people." Although other Black Washingtonians like former Armstrong High School student James Walker contended that stories similar to those of Chisley and the Martin's were "rare and far between," intraracial friction was a part of the everyday education of African Americans in the Black Divisions.

Howard University professor Kelly Miller's perspective on racial uplift represents at least one strand of Black elite thought on the nature of Black culture and identity for this period. It also gives a glimpse into additional reasons for friction between the Black elite and ordinary Blacks in Washington. Miller believed that ideas and strategies for the race came "from above and descend[ed] until it [met] the basis of popular needs, and then rebound[ed], bringing the concrete fulfillment up toward the level of the ideal from which it sprung."

One example of Miller's view was how he perceived the effect of the Great Depression on urban Black Americans, including Black Washingtonians. Miller argued that African Americans were "approaching the iron law of competition between White and Black labor…[w]here there is not work enough for all, the strong [Whites] will serve themselves first." With White intrusion in some of the lowest "Black jobs" such as barbering, waitering, and laundering, Miller believed that the "White man and his machine seem calculated to eliminate the Negro or to flatten him out at the bottom." This brought "the Negro's sad plight" as "surplus man…into full light." The passage of the National Recovery Act (NRA) and its minimum wage requirements under the New Deal had made it even easier for Black workers to be replaced by Whites, for the minimum was "deemed too high for the Black man." Miller declared that if "there be little hope in the domestic service from which we are being driven or in trade and manufacturing pursuits…the only remaining large scale occupation where race prejudice is least effective is on the farm." He also suggested that the "race slogan should be, if not 'Back to the Land,' at least 'Stay on the Land.'"

Miller's statement was a reflection of his analysis of Black plight and progress since the turn of the century. Miller wrote numerous editorials for Black weekly newspapers (including the *Washington Bee*, *Tribune*, and *Afro-American*) and articles for journals on African American success and failure. To say that Miller believed himself to be a cultured man who placed sincere hope in the American Dream and "had an unshakable faith that the only 'ism' that could end racial oppression and exploitation was Americanism" describes not only his beliefs but those of many Black elites in Washington and elsewhere. What can be said about Miller and many elite African Americans, in fact, is that they believed to a large extent that either Black culture would have to become more palatable to Whites or Blacks would have to become more "American" in order for the race to truly advance. It was the duty of the Black elite to show ordinary African Americans the way towards salvation for themselves and the race as a whole. Why else would Miller believe that movements based on sound ideas originated from the elite before trickling down to the masses?

One could also interpret Miller's trickle-down theory of Black intellectual and cultural development as egalitarian, as non-elite Blacks at least possessed the opportunity to mold elite ideas for their own purposes. But even if one acknowledges the validity of this interpretation, one must not forget that according to Miller, elite African American intellectuals are the ones who create and perfect ideas for all African Americans. There is no allowance for initial or final input from ordinary Blacks by Miller in this process; they can only react or respond to elite ideas. Miller refused to concede the possibility that the activities and ideas of ordinary African Americans could and did influence Black intellectual thought. Miller, moreover, could not envision that the everyday work of non-elites toward equality could occur *independent* of the intelligentsia. His article on the Great Depression and the Black migration to America's urban centers highlights the reality that everyday African Americans did impact Black intellectual production with their own perceptions and actions. Miller's statement exemplified his and the Black elite's disdain for ordinary Blacks in that he denied their ability to think and act independently of the Black elite.

Obviously the impact of circumstances external to the Black Washington community helped summon Miller's elitist response to the conditions African Americans faced during the 1930s. The continual migration of Blacks to the Nation's Capital and the Depression had a profound impact on the lives of African Americans in Washington, especially during the 1930s. Between 1910 and 1940, the Black population in Washington increased from 94,446 to 187,266, which translates to a ninety-eight percent growth rate over three decades. Well over half of this growth occurred during the 1930s, in which 55,198 African Americans added themselves to the city's population. Nearly 30,000 of those additional Blacks migrated to the Nation's Capital between 1930 and 1940. Widespread Black unemployment (it reached a high of forty-one percent in 1933) and underemployment and large numbers of urban Blacks on federal relief caused disillusionment among some Washington African Americans, while New Deal relief programs brought hope to many more and attracted thousands of unemployed Blacks to the city. In addition, most African Americans in Washington, similar to their counterparts in other cities in the first half of the twentieth century, worked as laborers and domestic servants (approximately two out of three by the early 1920s, as many as four out of five by 1930).

Non-elite Blacks in Washington and elsewhere attempted through organized protest to alleviate their economically-debilitating conditions in the 1930s, including involvement in the Communist Party. While most Black Washingtonians were not card-carrying members of the Communist Party, the reality that such a large number of African Americans migrated to the District in the midst of the greatest economic upheaval in this nation's history suggests protest and activity of an indirect nature. As historian James Grossman argued for an earlier generation of Black migrants, these new Black Washingtonians had "protested with their feet" their conditions of extreme poverty, discriminatory social services, and systematic joblessness. These attitudes, however hidden, were obvious enough for Miller to sound the alarm in his editorials about the plight of non-elite Blacks. This would explain in part his suggestion that urban Blacks should move back to rural areas in order to survive. Miller was not just worried that some Blacks would starve to death; he was also worried about the social structure of Black Washington being turned upside-down.

Black Washington was not alone in its experiences with intraracial friction and socioeconomic upheaval during the early and mid-twentieth century. From New York's Harlem to Pittsburgh's Hill District, from Chicago's South Side to Southern Alabama, intraracial fissures between Black elites and non-elites surfaced in numerous yet subtle ways. Not only did the elite establish exclusive clubs for themselves, they also established churches and other institutions to give them the physical and social space necessary to be with each other. Members of the urban Black elite were extremely protective of their status within the Black community, and feared that the migration of former sharecroppers to their communities would upset the delicate social balance, as well as their already limited influence among Whites. Rank-and-file members of Black communities—which in many cases included non-elite, lower middle class professionals—mostly feared that their lack of influence would deprive them of access to a good public education for their children and decent public services for their communities.

As Lawrence Otis Graham's *Our Kind of People* (1998) indicates, the Black elite of the early and mid-twentieth century was incestuous and protective by nature of its unusual status as leaders of a downtrodden people. Major demographic and cultural changes—such as the Great Migration, Harlem Renaissance, and the Great Depression—were typically viewed as threats to the elite's precious status. Graham's *Our Kind of People* is also a testimony to the reality that intraracial distinctions and frictions have endured among the Black elite into the twenty-first century.

The 1930s brought rapid school enrollment growth for both Blacks and Whites as a result of the influx of Black migrants and growth in Washington's overall population. The overall school population grew by about twenty-five percent between 1930 and 1938 For District Blacks, growth occurred at a much higher rate (thirty-six percent) than for Whites (twenty percent), particularly on the elementary school level. The higher growth rate among the Black school population occurred primarily because of the more rapid overall population increase among African Americans in Washington. The number of White elementary school children in D.C. Public Schools declined by roughly 1,000 between 1930 and 1938 (from 37,061 to 36,075, a three percent decline), while the number of Black elementary school children increased by about 4,600 (from 19,811 to 24,241, a twenty-two percent rise) during the same period. Although in terms of absolute numbers there was an equal increase in the number of Black and White students (approximately 10,000 apiece), Blacks made up about three-eighths of the total school population (37,000 out of 101,000).

This growth occurred in a school system that had been segregated into two divisions. The White and Black Divisions of D.C. Public Schools contained a total of 13 divisions, and each included one-thirteenth of the District's school population. The D.C. Board of Education categorized the White Divisions as Divisions 1-9, and the Black Divisions as Divisions 10-13. This system was constructed in 1906 with the assumption that African Americans students would never be more than thirty-one percent of the DC school population. Since the school system was segregated in terms of buildings, supplies, teachers, and students, an overcrowding problem developed during the 1930s.

By 1932, The *Washington Tribune* observed that the school board geared its building projects disproportionately toward the White divisions. The headline for one of the articles read: "With 34.92 Per cent of the School Population Negroes to Get 19.4 of the Buildings." The newspaper claimed that providing an inequitable number of new buildings for African American students at a time of growing enrollments had infuriated Black Washingtonians. The worries of 1932, though warranted, were temporarily alleviated the following year with the building of a new vocational school for boys on U Street (Cardozo High School). In the spring of 1935, the school board allowed construction on an elementary school, junior high school, and teacher's college in the Northeast and Southeast sections of the District.

Despite this construction, severe overcrowding continued for Blacks in the schools. With double-shift school days at some schools, student-teacher ratios as high as 44 to 1 (compared with 25 to 1 for Whites), and projections for even larger increases in the Black divisions by the early 1940s, the school board made a change in policy by transferring a previously White school into the Black division. In what would become a more common and controversial practice by the end of the Second World War, the DC School Board transferred an all-White elementary school to the Black Divisions in the early 1930s.

Funding for the D.C. Public Schools generally suffered during the 1930s which contributed to the overcrowding problem. While the number of students attending the public schools in the city increased by about 20,000 during the decade, school appropriations from the federal government did not keep pace. The school budget was cut from a high of $13.9 million in 1930 to $8.5 million by 1933. Between 1934 and 1940, federal school funding for the District increased from $9.8 million to $13.6 million, but declined between 1938 and 1940 (all in 1930s dollars). The reduction in funding appropriations effected the

Black divisions far worse than the rest of the city's schools. The largest cuts were in the areas of building projects and repairs for current infrastructure and grounds, areas which needed the most attention from the perspective of the Black community.

Garnet C. Wilkinson and the Black Divisions:

One cannot have a discussion of African American K-12 and adult public education in Washington during the 1920s and 1930s without mentioning Garnet C. Wilkinson. Wilkinson served as First Assistant Superintendent of the Black Divisions from 1921 to 1951. Prior to that, Wilkinson had been a teacher and principal at the M Street/Dunbar High School.

For the D.C. Public Schools, having Wilkinson in the second-highest position within the school administration was seen by many as the equivalent of having a Black person as superintendent over a predominantly African American school district today. Theoretically, the only forces with more authority over D.C. Public Schools were the Superintendent, who oversaw both the White and Black Divisions, and the D.C. School Board. Wilkinson exerted much influence over both the Superintendent and the School Board despite—or maybe because of—legal segregation, this because Wilkinson in effect represented the interests of 37,000 K-12 and adult students during the 1930s. That combined with the tradition of the School Board maintaining three African American members out of nine between 1906 and 1954 gave Wilkinson a higher degree of decision-making latitude than one would assume considering the circumstances.

At the same time, one also must note based on the state of Black education in the District that Wilkinson's authority had its limits. Segregation was as real for D.C. Public Schools as it was for any rural school district in the South, as overcrowded conditions and lack of school construction were constant reminders of systemic discrimination. The curriculum also never formally included the Black experience during Wilkinson's tenure. The overall Superintendent of Schools, the White Divisions' Superintendent, and six of nine D.C. Board of Education members were all White, meaning that any significant changes to the management of the Black Divisions could not occur without substantial White support. This kind of support was entirely unlikely under these segregated circumstances. One could even say that D.C. Public Schools practiced a form of "fair legal segregation" (or a "kinder, gentler" segregation) by allowing three Black board members and one White female member to serve on a board still controlled by White males. This arrangement would almost definitely calm any fears of further Black encroachment on the school board and in the school district administration, as they maintained this unofficial policy of board member selection through the 1940s. Once public sentiment towards this policy changed at the end of the 1940s, White school board members did become fearful of a loss of power over the school system.

Wilkinson's record as Superintendent of D.C. Public Schools' Black Divisions makes him an enigma. He simply does not fit neatly into any description as terms such as "elite Black," "race man," and "integrationist" would describe alone. Wilkinson was probably all of these terms and more. Wilkinson, for example, believed that "the entire colored school system was the best in the United States" because of its semi-autonomous status and because it prepared Black Washington's best and brightest for success and race work. But on more than one occasion, Wilkinson had also argued that more character education was needed for Black students in D.C. Public Schools. Although he thought that "the responsibility of character training is that of the home," Wilkinson also declared that "it is up to the school to supply whatever child development outside agencies fail to give."

Based on the given evidence, Wilkinson believed that it was a mistake to exclude the Black experience from D.C. Public School's formal curriculum. Wilkinson worked to supplement the curriculum through informal means. But Wilkinson also limited his commitment to the Black experience to the elite, meaning that most of his focus was on keeping Dunbar the best K-12 public school in the United States and on informal discussions about the contributions of great African Americans to American society. It was Wilkinson's belief that Dunbar's elite status would essentially raise the quality of the entire segregated Black system, and that anything tied to that promotion (especially achievements of Black Washington elites) would help prove to all that Blacks were the equals of Whites. This strategy—as documented by the late historian Nathan Huggins and David Levering Lewis regarding the Harlem Renaissance—lent itself to the goal of integration or assimilation, not to separatism or to multiculturalism.

Black Washington during the late-1920s and 1930s found itself struggling for answers to problems of poverty, wholesale unemployment, educational segregation, and exclusion. The nature of intrarace relations was also in a state of flux, with the addition of thousands of newcomers to the District and the transition of the old Black Washington elite to new demographics and conditions. This was also a watershed time period for attempting to find new solutions to these problems, and a chance for both elite and non-elite African Americans to engage in joint activities for the benefit of the community

Multiculturalism and Black Education in DC, 1925–40:

Most ordinary African Americans did not concern themselves with integration or assimilation. Everyday Black Washingtonians, while wanting to and knowing they needed to understand how to work "the system," also realized that the system was not about to include their experiences in the overall conversation about America. Most non-elite Blacks acknowledged that they would have to do that themselves, with some help from sympathetic Whites. While Wilkinson's perspective was certainly a part of Black elite thought in Washington, his example indicates the difficulty and the importance of understanding non-elite Black thought via activities on the cultural front. Because most working-class African Americans did not leave written records explaining their views of the elite, of education, and of their explorations of their African and American selves, most evidence of Black academic achievement is derived from the elite. This, of course, means that it is more important to examine non-elite Black actions and their interpretations of their actions in order to secure a fuller understanding of multiculturalism's history among African Americans. To be sure, some everyday Black Washingtonians involved in cultural activities such as Negro History Week could be considered nationalists or even Afrocentrists by today's standards. As evidenced by Wilkinson, a portion of African Americans in Washington believed in integration/assimilation. But it is also true that another group of Black Washingtonians believed in something more than separation or integration would allow.

This latter group included both members of the Black elite and working-class African Americans. Despite intraracial segregation and friction, prominent and ordinary African Americans did cooperate in the process of cultural exchange and self-discovery. Without some level of broad-based collaboration during these years in Washington and elsewhere, one could argue that the Civil Rights Movement of the subsequent generation would have only been an elite endeavor.

The most comprehensive way in which Black Washington dealt with issues of identity and race in the 1930s was through Negro History Week in February. For both the Black public schools and the Black community as a whole, Negro History Week was a month-long celebration, with plays, essay contests, speeches, and other activities heralding the contributions of African Americans to the community and to American society more generally. Negro History Week was the brainchild of Carter G. Woodson, the Harvard-educated "Father of African American History," who wanted to create a platform for Black children to learn more about Black history. Woodson had worked diligently in compiling research data and numerous articles on the African American experience between the completion of his doctoral studies in 1912 and the first Negro History Week in 1926. He was primarily interested in communicating the significance of the Black experience to younger Blacks through this program.

Woodson conceived Negro History Week to be a celebration of African American contributions to American society, an acknowledgment of the Black struggle for success and survival, and an education in the need for Black history as a vehicle for cultural renewal. Despite the constant carping over Negro History Week (which became Black History Month in 1976) being in February because it is the shortest month of the year (thus shortchanging Blacks), Woodson thought mid-February was the perfect week to celebrate Black history because it fell between Abraham Lincoln's and George Washington's birthdays. Superintendent Wilkinson and D.C. Public Schools took up Woodson's idea for a Negro History Week in the 1925–26 school year, making the school district the first to adopt the idea of celebrating the Black experience.

In February 1934, Howard history professor Charles Wesley, along with FDR "Black cabinet" member Robert Weaver (who advised on Black affairs in the Department of Interior), Woodson, and Howard Law School Dean Charles Houston gave speeches in honor of the week at Randall Junior High, Cardozo Night, Shaw Junior High, and Armstrong High Schools. Among the plays produced by these schools were "Two Races" and "The King's Dilemma," both showing the significance of Blacks and their activities in the development and growth of American society. Shaw Junior High School included an art exhibit that included "photographs of African art, creative illustrations based upon African art designed by Shaw pupils, and a collection of pictures showing outstanding Negroes and their achievements in creative arts, music, and the drama." At Browne Junior High School, "Negroes unknown by the average person were discussed by various members of the class," while at the Smothers School, Eugene K. Jones of the Commerce Department was the guest speaker, arguing that "our youth should be made to realize and feel that they are free and [should] carry themselves with confidence and self-assurance in all activities."

Teachers made important contributions to the activities of Negro History Week. At Armstrong Night High School, a presentation given by Mrs. E. H. Blake on "The Negro in Literature" included a short play and a discussion that involved Carter G. Woodson. Mrs. V. T. Turner, another teacher at Armstrong, performed a presentation titled "Our Women in History," which involved a play and Julia West Hamilton, a Black member of the D.C. School Board, as guest speaker. As late as April, 1934, Armstrong High School teachers presented a play meant to promote racial pride and self-respect in enabling Blacks to expect more out of their lives besides menial labor, titled "Come Out of the Kitchen." Part of the motivation for many Black teachers such as Turner and Hamilton included a implicit promotion of Black *women* as major contributors to the advancement of Black America and American society as a whole. Certainly the play "Come Out of the Kitchen" was geared to destroying the image of "Aunt Jemima," which not only is a racial stereotype, but is one that works only when combined with the belief in a docile Black woman who cares more about her White mistress' children than her own. Roughly sixty-five percent of all Black teachers in D.C. Public Schools during the 1930s were women, which added a gendered dimension to their activities and ideas that would lend themselves to multiculturalism.

For Black women teachers, it made sense not only to use Negro History Week as a means to infuse students with racial pride to erase the badge of inferiority, but also to dispel the stereotypes of African American women as either "Aunt Jemima" or "Jezebel." While Aunt Jemima was a docile and doughy Black woman, Jezebel was a sexually-promiscuous cesspool of immorality. This, of course, explains at least in part why the elite would attempt to nip in the bud any overt expression of materialism or sensuality shown by Black women in newspapers such as the *Washington Tribune*. These stereotypes would also certainly motivate teachers to confront images that could otherwise damage their own status and respectability.

Community centers in Black Washington also took part in the annual festivities, inviting clergy, church choirs, and prominent Blacks as speakers and entertainment for the week. Many of the community centers involved were located in Black neighborhoods in Southeast and Northeast DC with large working-class populations. According to the *Tribune*, the "interest in the communities has grown steadily since the original programs sponsored by Carter G. Woodson, Dr. Charles H. Wesley and Dr. Alaine [sic] Locke and this year surpassed all previous efforts." The newspaper also reported that civic associations and the Community Center Advisory Councils had given their full support in making the Negro History Week programs a success.

Along with other community centers, the Phillis Wheatley YWCA organized to observe Negro History Week, with an emphasis on African American musical contributions and performances. This YWCA invited Mrs. Hettie Anderson, the White general secretary of the K Street YWCA, as a guest speaker for an "Interracial and International program," evidence that both Black and White women saw Negro History Week as a significant event for the YWCA movement. More importantly, the Phillis Wheatley YWCA shows the high esteem Black Washingtonians held all community institutions when it came to a celebration of Black history, including those which involved White participants.

Churches in the Black Washington community also hosted meetings during Negro History Week, and in fact held meetings on African American history year-round. Among the Black churches involved throughout the 1930s were New York Avenue Presbyterian Church, Jerusalem Baptist Church, Fifteenth Street Presbyterian Church, Metropolitan AME Church, and Nineteenth Street Baptist Church. At Jerusalem Baptist Church, the church's pastor and other members of the congregation gave talks on "The Landing of the Negro in Jamestown," "The Negro Lawyer," "The Negro as a Citizen," and "The Negro as a Baptist" in their Negro History program in 1932. Lincoln Temple Church allowed Woodson and his Association for the Study of Negro Life and History (ASNLH) to use their building for their opening meeting in November 1933, where they held a special symposium on the future of African American education. The papers presented at this church appeared the following January in a special issue of the *Journal of Negro History*, which made clear that a number of Black intellectuals wanted to implement a curriculum that combined mainstream American and Black history and culture for the public schools.

Negro History Week and similar programs were meant to do far more than prove that African Americans were human beings capable of amazing achievements. These programs were meant to provide moral or "character training" for D.C. Public School students, to help create a sense of unity and cohesion in the community, and, most importantly, to provide a means by which Blacks in Washington could overcome obstacles that they faced both within and outside the community. Though a *Tribune* editorial asked the questions "Of what real service are our public schools?" and "Are we getting our money's worth out of our public schools?," African Americans in D.C. Public Schools used the school system as a training ground for considering issues of race consciousness and handling racism. Along with Divisions 10-13 of the District schools, community centers, churches, and other community organizations made Negro History Week a year-round undertaking during the 1930s. These programs encouraged innovative thinking on the part of teachers, students, community organizers, and members of the Black Washington working-class as a whole.

Students and teachers commented on what took place in the educational process around issues of training, culture, and race. Students in Dunbar High School's Negro History Club believed that it was necessary to "Keep Abreast With the Time" through frequent discussions of "Negro contemporaries" and issues of race. Walker Savoy, the principal of Garnet-Patterson Junior High

School, stated that it was his job "to sacrifice [his] own personal progress and ele-
vate, instead, Garnet-Patterson" and its Black students, "molding student person-
alities through co-ordination of school services around general social and civic
development." Savoy's views were typical of Black elites and those aspiring non-
elites who believed in race uplift, if one buys Gaines' and Kelley's arguments
about Black elite ideals of thrift and self-serving sacrifice for the "struggle" or the
"cause."

By the 1930s, the directors of the Junior NAACP of Washington, DC created
programs to instill a sense of racial pride in the pre-adult members of the Branch.
One of the director's reports noted that at their meetings they had created scrap-
books that contained articles about African American accomplishments in America and abroad. Their meetings also routinely consisted of discussions of topics
based on Woodson's work in Black history. In addition, their Juniors, with the
help of the YWCA, produced plays dealing with issues of race and culture, plays
that the Junior directors argued "were put over with a success." A motto was even
created for the Junior, which reflected Black thought on respectability and cultural pluralism during the 1930s:

> No man is superior to me simply because he is White,
> No man is inferior to me because he is Black,
> He alone is my superior in character, mentality, and attainments,
> He alone is my inferior who is inferior in these things.

This motto suggests that African Americans simply deserve respect and equality because they are part of the *human* race. Whites who did not treat Blacks as
equals would be inferior because of their limited "content of character."

And although one might be tempted to interpret the motto as Black elite chest
thumping, remember the first two lines of the motto. If one infers from them,
then the District Junior NAACP (or at least the author(s) of the motto) was also
suggesting that "no man is superior to me because he is *part of an elite class*," for
those who would believe this would lack the "character" necessary to look beyond
the superficial (such as skin color). The motto might as well say "judge one inferior or superior only by the content of their character, by their level of knowledge
and wisdom, and by what they have accomplished through these valuable
attributes." This, without a doubt, is a key tenet of multiculturalism, that regardless of race, ethnicity, gender, or culture, every person and cultural group has an
equal footing on the world stage.

Individual Black Washingtonians who grew up during the era expressed a variety of opinions on how the community brought them into contact with the African American experience and issues of race and culture. Felicia Chisley stated that although she could not recall exactly when she first learned about the Black experience in school, she did know that "all of those things [regarding race pride] were instilled in us," and that this "was done subtly...it wasn't as overt as it is now." When Chisley was in school, some of her knowledge of the Black experience came because "we knew who Carter G. Woodson was, because he started Negro History [Week], and it was right here in D.C. We knew some things because of where we were." As a result of Black pride, history, and culture being "infused in [her] life," Chisley maintained that "[w]e were taught, and we were taught much better, believe me, much better" than either her White counterparts in the 1930s or Black District children today. Certainly some of Chisley's comments have a hint of nostalgia, but they also point to her half-century in D.C. Public Schools as a student, teacher, and administrator before and after segregation's end.

Chester Martin's high school education took place in Dunbar during the early 1930s, where discussions of Black contributions to American history and culture took place in the midst of intraracial problems. Mr. Martin remembered that "if...somebody...mention[ed] the air brake used on the train, right away, the teacher would tell us that [it] was invented by a Black man...when the subject would come up, why, if Blacks had anything to do with it, we'd talk about it." Mr. Martin also reflected about his Negro History Week experiences, recalling that "[e]very now and then we have assemblies, and they'd have recitals, and there would be Blacks, former graduates of Dunbar, and they would come back and make talks and presentations, so we were constantly reminded of what Blacks had done and what Blacks were doing."

These experiences also illuminate the reality that Dunbar was the creme de la creme of D.C. Public Schools' Black Divisions. Chester Martin's comments on being reminded of "what Blacks had done and what Blacks were doing" is true except when one compares them to his previous comments about many speakers being former Dunbar students. Of course other schools such as the more pedestrian Armstrong High School (which primarily provided vocational training for its Black students) conducted assemblies, speeches, and activities during Negro History Week and throughout the year on the Black experience. Dunbar, though, made it a point to bring back its graduates to show that they considered their current students valuable to the future of the Black community. To be sure, these activities instilled race pride and faith. But this faith was at least based partly in arrogance, assuming that the future of the race in Washington depended primarily on Dunbar's students.

James Walker, another native Black Washingtonian who went through D.C. Public Schools in the 1930s and 1940s, noted that in elementary school "[w]e were taught that you didn't stand on the street corner. We were taught to hold our heads high and to try to strive above the achievements that had been made by the generation that preceded us." Walker felt that "we [Blacks] had an obligation to pass this on to our own children." Because of his schooling and despite his working-class background, Walker also "felt that [he] had a lot of exposure" to the Black and the mainstream American experiences.

In recounting her high school experiences in race relations in the late-1920s and early 1930s, Enez Martin remarked that she "didn't know when we didn't have Black history!" Although Mrs. Martin attended St. Francis, a Catholic high school in Baltimore, it was also a segregated experience. The all-female school was run by an order of Black nuns. Mrs. Martin's experiences were similar to her husband's: "I don't know when we didn't have Black history, because anything that we were studying, if in any way tied in with Negroes, Africans, whatever, we were taught that was where it tied in." Mrs. Martin's classes, like her husband's, intertwined the African American experience with the history and culture of mainstream America. St. Francis was not so "cued in to...our own people to such an extent that everything else was excluded" according to Mrs. Martin. Both Martin's benefitted from the fact that their teachers informally taught Black history and culture side-by-side with the White American experience during the 1930s. Whether at Dunbar, another school in the D.C. Black Divisions, or enrolled in a Catholic school, Chisley, Walker, and the Martin's all saw the importance of Black history and culture through their teachers' informal instruction. The "curriculum" for what their teachers taught on the Black experience did not originate from the D.C. Board of Education, nor would it until 1969.

Howard University was another institution within the Black Washington community that infused its students with "a sense of racial pride." Or, at least, its students were also interested in issues of racial uplift and autonomy. Howard University, like the other institutions in the Black Washington community, observed Negro History Week on an annual basis. Kelly Miller's and Alain Locke's attempts to set up a National Negro Library and Museum at Howard were well received by both their colleagues and students. Among others, Charles Wesley and Benjamin Brawley both came out as the most prominent Howard faculty in support of the idea. Wesley, who served as chair of Howard's history department from 1921 to 1941, had created a number of new courses, including ones in "Negro American" and African history. Wesley started an African history program at Howard, "the first such program offered in an American or European university." Though an English professor by training, Brawley did extensive writing in Black history during the 1920s and 1930s. Both Wesley and Brawley had a personal stake in supporting the museum project.

For Black philosophy and African art critic Locke, this library and museum would "emphasize the Negro, first, in the United States; second, in other parts of North and South America, the West Indies, and islands of special interest to us; and third, as far as possible, in Europe and the African background" in order to "bring together" a variety of documents "pertaining to Negroes of prominence in any walk of life." The Moorland-Spingarn Research Center at Howard University was the direct result of the efforts of Miller, Locke, other faculty, and the student council. Howard officials saw the Moorland-Spingarn Research Center as the depository for Black history and culture, and, in effect, a depository of racial pride.

Unlike many of the other major institutions in the community, Howard was an almost exclusively Black elite and middle class endeavor which possessed an extra privilege and responsibility as the "Capstone of Negro Education." When Virginia McGuire—the president of the NAACP—D.C. Branch and a soon-to-be member of the D.C. Board of Education—argued that the "group needs education and economic sufficiency," she also implied that Howard students were the "coming generation of leaders" who would provide all Blacks with this educational and economic competency.

McGuire urged Howard students to develop "a definite plan, followed by concerted action" and "courageous leadership" in effectively meeting the needs of the Black Washington community and beyond. Although Black leadership in other community gatherings discussed African American history and their contributions to American society, as well as their own plans for the community's betterment, Howard students were the ones given the monumental responsibility of leading Blacks to a better life, which points to the bias of status within Black Washington. Despite all the efforts of churches, a variety of community centers, the activities of students and teachers in D.C. Public Schools, it was Howard's students who alone were expected to take up the mantle of race work and successfully revamp the community and overcome the racist ills of the larger society. Although there were times and activities in which both Black elites and ordinary African Americans interacted on issues of race, culture, and education, for the Howard community, the elites were in charge of race work and set the terms for that discussion.

Or so McGuire and the leadership at Howard thought. The aforementioned experiences regarding Negro History Week and related events suggest otherwise. These Negro History Week and related experiences indicate that non-elite Blacks did not automatically assume that prominent African Americans were in control of the race's destiny. They also imply that some elite and working-class Blacks recognized the need to bridge the intraracial divide for the purposes of cultural discovery, interaction, and shaping the African American "walk by faith."

Critics argue that fishing for examples of multiculturalism among everyday African Americans is "ahistorical" and "anachronistic," especially since the term is loaded with "post-modern" connotations. African American scholars in particular would argue that what we are describing here is a precursor to what we now know as Afrocentricity, not multiculturalism. Surely Black Washingtonians did not have the time, luxury, or inclination to understand Whites or mainstream America. A different and less skeptical perspective of multiculturalism is one that accounts for the context of how teachers and community leaders introduced programs such as Negro History Week to Black Washington and elsewhere. These programs are much more than mere precursors of Afrocentricity.

The key question at this point must be how relevant these activities are to understanding multiculturalism in today's climate. Some would probably argue that the activities of some elite and ordinary African Americans in Washington during the late 1920s and the 1930s, even if they do add up to multiculturalism, are irrelevant to the nature of multiculturalism today. Detractors would declare that times have changed, and that multiculturalism as a philosophy adheres to more than race and class issues. Those critics would be correct in also noting that while most of the actors in this story were certainly not conscious of multiculturalism or cultural pluralism, many African Americans and other Americans today are aware of the term and its potential implications.

This is, of course, exactly the point regarding Black cultural/educational activities during the 1930s. It is because many within the Black Washington community were not conscious of all the implications that one can read into their activities today that makes them so important. The other major counterargument to potential critics is that it is not at all clear what the *practice* of multiculturalism looks like today, much less its actual definition. In practice, multiculturalism involved interaction between African Americans in Washington regardless of class, age, gender, and skin tone. Multiculturalism in this context also involved some cooperation on the part of White Washingtonians, surprising considering segregation and White beliefs of Black inferiority during the early-twentieth century.

Certainly some Black elites and scholars who were engaged in this process saw ordinary African Americans as unequal players, believing that they were enlightening their disadvantaged counterparts in the great achievements of African America. And there also were everyday Blacks seeking enlightenment from their more prominent peers in the fight against exclusion. But similar to the realization that gray existed between the Black of nationalism and the White of assimilation, non-elite Blacks were active participants in Negro History Week and corresponding events. They apparently thought about the implications of these activities, as was the case with Chisley, the Martins, and James Walker. Seven decades after these events occurred, these men and women discussed how important it was for them to participate in these activities, specifically how these activities prepared them to be African American in a society dominated by widespread segregation and discrimination. They knew who they were, and they knew what society they lived in, and were ready to meet the challenges of both realities.

All of this is highly relevant for our current discourse on multiculturalism, as many would assume that American education continues to perform very poorly in the cultural preparation of all students for our society. African Americans in particular would claim that this is all too true. Scholars and the most prominent members of American society continue to assume that knowledge trickles down to the masses, discounting the abilities of ordinary citizens to create knowledge and participate in serious dialogue about important issues. Successful African Americans in American society and in academia have not been immune to this kind of thinking. To slightly misquote a common phrase, the "main thing" in 1930 continues to be the "main thing" in 2004. African Americans continue to struggle to define themselves in a society they perceive as hostile to their actions, with inner struggles between elite and everyday Blacks over the details of that definition. The one variable that has changed is that there is far less interaction between scholars and non-elite African Americans over these issues than there was during the 1930s, especially during the past four decades.

The issue of leadership remains a fundamental tension among African Americans. Who should lead? Who has the right to lead? Should Blacks invest themselves in chosen leadership, or should Blacks *make* themselves leaders? Many of the problems in Black Washington and elsewhere in the last quarter of the twentieth century stem from the lack of clear answers to these questions. If elite Blacks assumed a right to leadership and non-elite African Americans assumed that they should be led by prominent Blacks, no tension would exist. Leaders, Black,

White, or otherwise, are born *and* made, rather than chosen based on family pedigree. Today, unfortunately, leadership and status in African America are based on family pedigree and one's proximity to the Civil Rights Movement's leadership. To put it bluntly, leadership in recent decades has been determined by how one answers the question "Did you march with Martin Luther King?" There has always been a fundamental flaw in the Black elite's conception of leadership as a quality one is granted by others instead of an intangible quality one earns. Whether leaders become as famous as Martin Luther King or remain buried in obscurity, they almost always choose themselves rather than allow themselves to be chosen by a "Committee of Elite Correctness." In exploring the socioeconomic and cultural transformations of the last third of the twentieth century, one must at least consider why good leaders are difficult to come by these days.

4

Looking Forward to the Past: Black Washington and Multiculturalism's Impact

It was Wednesday, June 10, 1987, my last day in Mount Vernon High School. The day was a complete blur of "goodbyes" to friends and teachers and "good riddance" to some classmates and my guidance counselor. After my last class that afternoon, I walked down the second floor steps and the first floor halls of the high schools to my locker one more time. While clearing out my locker, the head of the Science Department walked by and asked to meet with me. I went over to her office, and for the next fifteen minutes, she proceeded to explain to me how much of a disappointment I was while a student at Mount Vernon High School.

The Science Department chair claimed that I had underachieved throughout my four years as a student, that I should have been ranked in the top ten of my class (I ranked fourteenth out of 545 students), and that my performance in Advanced Placement (AP) Physics class this past year was beyond abominable. All I could focus on was the amount of anger and emotion she possessed in her voice and eyes. One would have thought that I had been expelled from school or had committed a heinous crime considering her distaste for me.

There were two particularly odd things the Science Department head said during her attack on my character. One was that I had let down the Black students of the school and the Mount Vernon Black community by not finishing closer to the top of my class. I guess I did let my Black classmates down. I only ranked second in grade point average among Black males and eighth among all African Americans and Afro-Caribbeans in my graduating class.

The other statement she made really surprised me. She told me: "You don't have any excuses! There is nothing going on at home that could justify your performance." When I disagreed, the Science department head's face turned stern. She said that nothing occurring in my life would ever compare to the problems

Blacks faced back in the 1960s. Besides, she "marched with Dr. Martin Luther King." What could I possibly say to that? Her statement was not only irrelevant to the browbeating session, but dumb considering how often African Americans over the age of forty had wrapped themselves in the rhetoric of the Civil Rights movement by the late-1980s. My thought after her statement was "Who *didn't* march with Martin Luther King during the 1950s and 1960s?" Based on these statements and the numerous other ones I had heard growing up about marching with Martin Luther King, it seemed to me that every African American was out singing "We Shall Overcome" instead of working, raising their families, or going to school. Afterwards, I left the Science head's office angry and bewildered, yet happy, realizing that I would never have to see her again.

Aside from realizing that some of America's educators have idiotic ideas about motivating students, this incident points to the issue of nostalgia among many African Americans regarding the Civil Rights era versus the problems Blacks face today. Many Americans these days feel that America's greatest years of peace and prosperity occurred immediately before the turbulent 1960s. Some Americans believe that whatever the problems of American society before the 1960s, they pale in comparison with the complex conundrums that the society has been confronted with over the last four decades. This is particularly true in American education, where nostalgia for an allegedly simpler past has run amok in recent years. The push for a return to the basics of reading, writing, and arithmetic via the No Child Left Behind (NCLB) Act and for locally-controlled public schools are among the demands of those who long for the so-called good-ole-days in American education.

Some Americans—Black as well as White—also believe that education for African Americans was better when schools were legally segregated than in the current post-Civil Rights climate. This notion is especially strong for many Black Washingtonians who remember when D.C. Public Schools, the Black Divisions, and the elite mecca Dunbar High School were considered some of the best schools in America. Despite segregation, systematic discrimination, the almost total exclusion of the Black experience from the formal curriculum, not to mention intraracial exclusion within the Black Division through Dunbar, many Black Washingtonians now see this period as the zenith of education in the District.

This basic fact certainly does not mean that Black Washingtonians with even the vaguest memories of life before the 1960s are longing for the glory days of heartbreaking discrimination and inequality. These men and women instead recognize that the magic wand of desegregation did not eliminate poverty, inequitable distribution of services, or necessarily provide a better education for themselves or their children. As a character in law professor Derrick Bell's *Faces at the Bottom of the Well* (1992) explained it, desegregation is just another example of what "Black folks work for and White folks grant when they realize—long before we do—that it is mostly a symbol that won't cost them much and will keep us Blacks pacified." Whether they are entirely conscious of it or not, it is a safe bet that many working-class and poor African American Washingtonians in particular believe that desegregation helped create new and more complex problems, while only giving them a symbol of a level playing field.

Certainly Black Washingtonians are not alone in their assessment of school desegregation and in their insistence for a curriculum which includes the Black experience as a fundamental component. The story of Black Washington's coping with demographic shifts in population and with a failing urban education system since 1960 is really America's story. "The DC Story" is intended to represent, at least in part, the related experiences of African Americans throughout the country between 1960 and the early 1990s, whether one resided in New York City, San Francisco, Bradley, Arkansas, or rural Utah. "The DC Story" of overcrowded schools, segregation, resegregation, poor school achievement, the fight for inclusive curricula, and the Black generation gap has and continues to affect all Whites, Blacks, and Browns this side of World War II.

One of the common threads between the 1930s and the post-1960s period has been the push for inclusion of the Black experience in the D.C. Public Schools' formal curriculum. This has been another way of "looking forward to the past," in that some African Americans expected the inclusion of African ancestors/African American historical achievements to raise the level of positive self-esteem and educational achievement among Black students. And just like in the 1930s, understanding the different perspectives of Black Washingtonians on these issues plays an important role in understanding how American society as a whole should examine multiculturalism, Afrocentricity, and assimilation. This chapter involves a discussion of the large-scale forces and events that have affected Black Washington since 1960, as well as the activities of District African Americans to change the D.C. Public School curriculum. The differing perspectives of older elite Blacks and their non-elite (and in some cases, younger) counterparts regarding the Black Washington community and culture are also examined here, especially regarding their amnesia (excuse me, nostalgia) for the past. Fear is also relevant here, for with the present bleakness of conditions for ordinary Blacks—and no hope of substantial improvement in the future—many look to the past for examples of success in the midst of misery (e.g., the Civil Rights/Black Power movements) and for examples of past glory (e.g., Afrocentricity).

Prelude: Desegregation and D.C. Public Schools, 1940–60:

In order to understand the changes that occurred in Black Washington, D.C. Public Schools, and the city of Washington itself after 1960, one must briefly examine the period between 1940 and 1960. This period represents a watershed in the history of African Americans in the city of Washington. Through interracial and intraracial cooperation, the system of Jim Crow that had dominated the city for the better part of a century crumbled after only a decade and a half of constant pressure. In the years immediately following the *Brown v. Board of Education* and *Bolling v. Sharpe* decisions (1954) declaring segregation unconstitutional in the states and Washington, D.C. respectively, the desegregation strategy was fully implemented without a serious hitch.

The year 1947 was pivotal, for a number of different events occurred that made desegregation the key issue for both Black and White Washingtonians. The issue of overcrowding in the Black Divisions of D.C. Public Schools came to a head in 1947, when Daisy Carr of the Browne Junior High School and the NAACP—D.C. Branch took D.C. Public Schools to court for its practice of administratively transferring dilapidated nineteenth-century buildings from the White Divisions to the Black Divisions. Carr's school had a total capacity for 888 students, but 1,707 were enrolled by the 1946–47 school year. She attempted to transfer to a White school near her neighborhood and the D.C. School Board refused to allow it based on the nearly 80 years of legal school segregation in the District. Carr and the NAACP—D.C. Branch claimed that segregation ultimately caused the overcrowding at Browne and called for the desegregation of the school system. It would take until 1950 for the *Carr* case to be resolved in favor of Carr and the NAACP—D.C. Branch, but an additional four years passed before the school system desegregated. Of course, school overcrowding was one of the key factors in forcing schools throughout the U.S. to desegregate during the 1960s and 1970s, because overcrowding crystalized the reality of an inequitable distribution of resources by race.

At the same time the *Carr* case took shape, the D.C. School Board's refused to allow a "White" student to attend a Black school. Karla Galarza, a Mexican American high school student, wanted to transfer from the Burdick Vocational School in the White Divisions to the Margaret Murray Washington Vocational School in the Black Divisions because the Black school provided better training for fashion design. Despite pleas from Galarza's father, Superintendent Corning and the School Board refused the transfer because Galarza was not Black. Galarza was labeled "White" more out of convenience than reality, which pointed to yet another problem with the District's segregated system.

The discovery of a dehumanizing version of the children's book *Little Black Sambo* generated the most protests from the Black Washington community. The original version of *Little Black Sambo*, published by British author Helen Bannerman in 1899, was designed to portray Black and Asian Indian characters as positive and crafty ones. The American edition being used in D.C. Public Schools, however, portrayed African Americans as Step 'n Fetchit, big-lipped, big-grinned, happy-go-lucky imbeciles. What especially irked District African Americans about the book was the use of the term "Sambo," a derogatory term on par with "nigger" and "pickaninny." It also did not help that *Little Black Sambo* ended with the character having outsmarted a tiger only to gleefully sit down and devour a stack of pancakes.

A storm of controversy erupted on the pages of the *Washington Post* and *Washington Afro-American* in the fall of 1947 after the NAACP—D.C. Branch sent a letter to the D.C. School Board demanding the removal of *Little Black Sambo* from the D.C. Public School reading list. It turned out, ironically enough, that the book was not on the school district's reading list. Whites accused Black Washingtonians of being "humorless" and uppity, while Blacks accused White Washingtonians of prejudice and bigotry fueled by segregation. The *Post* published an arrogant rebuke of an editorial against the Black Washington community, condemning them for "damaging a good cause by pressing it to the point of absurdity." *Afro-American* editor Ralph Matthews countered the *Post's* editorial with one of his own, writing that there are "those who…think it important that this heritage be understood in order to use it as a basis for continuing the dual system from generation to generation."

If this sounds anything like the 1998 controversy in New York City over a White elementary school teacher using the book *Nappy Hair* in her classroom, then one would be mixing apples and oranges in terms of race and protest. In the pre-Civil Rights era climate of the late-1940s, books that depicted Blacks as stupid and docile were commonplace, and African Americans knew which books these were. In the *Nappy Hair* incident, parental protests were based in ignorance, as many had never seen or read the book. City school officials overreacted to the protests out of a distorted view of political correctness. And of course, there was the reality that a *White* woman was teaching *Black* children about the values of Black culture, which was at the heart of the controversy. *Nappy Hair* is a story about an African American girl who decides to be proud of her hair, not about acting like a buffoon in order to please bigoted Whites, which is the point of the

Americanized version of *Little Black Sambo*. In any case, by the end of 1947, the NAACP—D.C. Branch and Black Washington as a whole had begun an all-out effort to end segregation, which culminated in the 1954 *Bolling v. Sharpe* decision.

Not all groups within the District African American community participated equally in the movement to desegregate the school district and the city. Prominent Black Washingtonians had the largest stake in making desegregation a reality, as they led the charge with pickets, lawsuits, and local organizations formed solely to fight segregation. The activities of prominent Blacks within the NAACP—D.C. Branch such as civil rights lawyers William Hastie and Doxey Wilkerson and educator/activist Mary Church Terrell stood out from other individuals and organizations in the city. As a branch indirectly linked to the policies of the NAACP National Office (led by Walter White, Roy Wilkins, Charles Houston, and Thurgood Marshall), the D.C. Branch carried out much of New York's desegregation strategy. Prior to 1947, the Branch made some adaptations to the National Office's strategy that involved organizing intercultural education and cultural and educational programs in the public schools and in the Black community as a whole. After 1947, the Branch and most elite Black Washingtonians had aligned themselves primarily with desegregation as the ultimate panacea for the ills of Black schooling and the African American community.

Desegregation would not have succeeded without the support of a substantial proportion of the Black community at large. Examples of working and middle class Black Washingtonians participating in pickets, sending letters to newspapers, and joining local organizations to fight segregation exist throughout this period. Desegregation also gained legitimacy among African American Washingtonians because it created opposition from the White community, especially since Black leaders were visible in their work for desegregation. Rank-and-file members of the Black middle and working-classes did not put all of their proverbial eggs in the basket of desegregation as *the* strategy for race advancement. While many in both classes supported desegregation, they also participated in everyday activities that promoted an informal version of race pride and multiculturalism in the public schools and in Black Washington. A number of prominent District African Americans supported the development of these ideas, most notably among them Alain Locke before his death in 1954.

Problems of overcrowding in the Black Divisions of the District schools mounted as Whites moved out of the city and the school district began to consider a desegregation plan. By the time the NAACP—D.C. Branch filed what would become the *Bolling* decision in 1952, the D.C. Board of Education had already begun to study desegregation as a possible solution to its problem. By the time of the decision in May 1954, however, no report on the benefits of desegregation in solving the overcrowding problem had been completed. One study found that "the Board never discussed desegregation in any aspect, nor instructed the Superintendent to produce any material on desegregation showing its consequences for budget, curriculum and overcrowding" in the two-year period between 1952 and the *Brown* decision. D.C. Public Schools was almost totally unprepared for the physical desegregation of the school system, despite the fact that for at least two years (and when one accounts for protests by Black Washingtonians, since 1947), the Board knew that the status quo was coming to an end.

No sooner did the desegregation forces defeat the evil kingdom of segregation than other problems such as overcrowding become more obvious. For District African Americans, the period between 1940 and 1960 brought major demographic changes. By 1960, Blacks had become the majority of Washington's population (fifty-four percent), growing from 187,255 in 1940 to 411,737 in 1960. About 72,000 African Americans migrated to the District from various parts of the United States, particularly the South. Starting in the early 1950s, the White Washington population began a decline that continued until the gentrification of the late-1990s. After reaching a high of 517,865 in 1950, the White Washington population declined by 172,597 to about 345,268 by 1960. Many of these District Whites moved to the suburban counties surrounding Washington. Joined by Whites who moved directly into suburban Washington, the overall population of Montgomery and Prince George's Counties, Maryland, and Fairfax and Arlington Counties in Virginia grew at a rapid pace. Between 1940 and 1960, 832,000 Whites contributed to a total increase of 865,355 in the four counties, with a population increase of 524,229 Whites during the 1950s alone. Fairfax County, Virginia's population explosion was the most significant, as its White population grew from 40,929 in 1940, to 98,557 in 1950, and to 275,002 in 1960. The White population in Montgomery and Prince George's Counties in Maryland grew by 250,000 apiece during the 1940s and 1950s. The Second World War and the immediate post-war period intensified the migration/suburbanization process, as the federal government expanded its operations into suburban Washington. This, along with real estate and banking policies that favored Whites, attracted large numbers of Whites and white-collar businesses to the suburbs. These same trends obviously occurred in urban communities throughout the U.S., reformulating cities such as Baltimore, Detroit, Chicago, New York, Philadelphia, and Oakland as ebony in nature, and creating ivory-White suburbs outside of these urban centers.

The migration of thousands of African Americans into the city and Whites into the suburbs between 1954 and 1960 led to significant resegregation in the District school. One study of the first five years after desegregation found that about "one half of the schools desegregated in 1954 were located in [census] tracts showing substantial Black residence in 1950" (some seventy-five percent Black). The other schools were in census tracts that were less than twenty-five percent Black in 1950 but were more than fifty percent African American by 1960; schools in these tracts resegregated the fastest. The twin trends of the "Chocolate City" and "Vanilla flight" made it impossible for D.C. Public Schools to desegregate by the early 1960s.

D.C. Public Schools in Turmoil, 1960–Present:

The process of desegregation in D. C. Public Schools did not end with the 1950s, primarily because the same forces that had forced Black Washingtonians to protest *for* desegregation had also caused the schools to *re*segregate. One Howard University study showed that between 1954 and 1956, de jure (or legal) segregation became de facto (or default) segregation, as White parents either enrolled their children in private or parochial schools, or transferred them to the remaining predominantly White schools in the District. Educator Beverly Reid estimated that as much as ten percent of the District's White population (roughly 50,000) left the city for the suburbs less than a year after the school district began the desegregation process. Washington by 1956 was the first major American city to experience what became a national trend: central cities that are majority Black or non-White (or "majority-minority") with suburban areas that are almost as White as the driven snow. Whites who remained in the District typically were not of school age, so as time passed, there were fewer and fewer Whites in D.C. Public Schools. The growth of Black Washington, on the other hand, made the school system almost exclusively African American. D.C. Public Schools reached its peak enrollment years in the 1967–69 period, when about ninety-four percent of the nearly 150,000 students were Black. White student enrollment had declined from 51,278 in 1951, to 24,000 in 1960, and again to a little bit less than 10,000 seven years later. The number of African Americans in D.C. Public Schools rose from almost 51,000 in 1951 to 98,000 in 1960, and to nearly 140,000 by 1967.

By 1967, a lawsuit brought against D.C. Public Schools by activist Julius Hobson for its *de facto* segregation led to another ruling ordering the school board to desegregate. Hobson, a Black civil rights activist, had fought since the late-1950s to force the public schools to come up with more permanent plans for integrating Black and White students in the District. With the backing of liberal Whites, Hobson brought a lawsuit against Superintendent Carl Hansen and D.C. Public Schools. The case became known as *Hobson v. Hansen* and was the height of ten tumultuous years (1958–67) of change for the embattled Hansen, who had presided over most of D.C. Public School's desegregation transition. The *Hobson* case was decided by Judge J. Skelly Wright of the U. S. District Court for the District of Columbia, who had a reputation for making liberal rulings on issues of racial discrimination. Wright concluded that the "scholastic achievement of the disadvantaged child, Negro and White, is strongly related to the racial and socio-economic composition of the student body of his school. A racially and socially integrated school environment increases the scholastic achievement of the disadvantaged child of whatever race." Wright ordered that busing take place between the overcrowded Black schools and the underpopulated White schools west of Rock Creek Park in the Northwest section of the District.

In the aftermath of the *Hobson* decision, Carl Hansen attacked Judge Wright for his "admitted" lack of experience in issues of school administration. Hansen saw the notion of de facto segregation as one that D.C. Public Schools could not change. From Hansen's perspective, Wright's decision was both a judicial overstep of authority and impossible to enforce. Hansen also complained about Julius Hobson's involvement as the main plaintiff in the case, calling him a "Caesar," an "Uncle Tom of the worst sort," and a "Black voice speaking the words of his White masters." Hansen finally resigned as Superintendent in the summer of 1967 after a long battle to remain in his post, which he lost as a result of the *Hobson* decision and his steady stream of prejudiced pontifications.

The other major issue raised by Hansen and the *Hobson* decision was student achievement. In addition to the busing order, Wright mandated the abolition of the formal four-track, ability grouping program that Hansen and the D.C. School Board implemented in 1956. Hansen had personally constructed the four-track system when serving as D.C. Public Schools' Deputy Superintendent of Senior High Schools from 1955 to 1958. So it should be no surprise that he would declare that those who were against ability grouping were either "theorists who have never taught a day in their lives" or "Negroes [insecure] about desegregation (particularly 'civil rightists')." Hansen saw the Civil Rights Movement as the main cause of the four-track system's downfall. Only Hansen and the District school teachers realized "how impossible it is to teach highly diverse pupils." What all of this says is that Hansen believed that most African Americans lacked White intellectual capabilities. Beyond that, Hansen might have been seeking to create a system that educators would call a magnet program today, in which high-achieving White students would attend D.C. Public Schools with the approval of leery parents.

As historian Stephen Diner has shown in his work on D.C. Public Schools, concern about ability grouping and other issues dealing with student achievement began to develop in the post-1945 period. Diner argued that a growing concern over achievement issues among Washingtonians led to a "crisis of confidence" that spread like a plague among all connected to D.C. Public Schools, which also led to the system's poor reputation by the 1970s. Diner noted that as early as the 1949 Strayer Report, ample evidence existed concerning declines in student achievement. George Strayer, who served as a statistician for D.C. Public Schools between 1928 and 1930, found that "[l]arge numbers of pupils enter the junior high schools ill-prepared for the work on this level because of inadequate preparation in basic skills."

With desegregation in 1954 came increasing scrutiny of scholastic achievement in D.C. Public Schools, along with the major transformations in the city's demographics and political culture. Whether they were "segregationists…politicians, educational policy analysts, activists, reformers, and journalists" all had their own reasons to discredit D.C. Public Schools, creating a divisive atmosphere in the community and in the institution. Diner found that a small trickle of articles on allegedly new problems in student achievement began to flow from Washington's White newspapers and national magazine articles during the late-1950s and 1960s, including a 1956 *U.S. News & World Report* article "Do Mixed Schools Lower Classroom Standards?" The stream turned into a muddy, flooding river of test scores that declined every year from 1959 until the early-1970s, as well as more numerous Washington newspaper articles critical of D.C. Public Schools. The Passow Report (1967) examining the state of public education in Washington understated the situation a bit with its conclusion that "education in the District is in deep and probably worsening trouble."

The DC story flowed beyond its public schools to include the same problems of overcrowding, "White flight," Black migration, de facto segregation, and declining achievement in all of America's urban schools during the 1950s, 1960s, and 1970s. Politicians, pundits, and the press have all played up the failures of American K-12 education, and in the process linked these problems to desegregation. The assumption has been that since schools are no longer legally segregated, they serve as bastions of equality, particularly equality of opportunity. This so-called equality has been built on sands of fear, as "White flight" out of public schools and urban areas took with it not only White students, but also money, many of the best teachers, and a school system's reputation. It also created the implicit assumption that anything "Black" regarding neighborhoods and education was automatically inferior to the growing White suburban enclaves and their pristine schools.

It goes without saying that this process did not take a long period of time to evolve. Within two years of the *Brown* decision, *U.S. News & World Report* published their article describing the falling classroom standards of D.C. Public Schools and other "mixed" schools in urban America. Desegregation had barely been given time to breathe—much less work—before it became linked with failure. This, of course, was an expression of doubt, another manifestation of fear. Not only did administrators such as Hansen doubt that desegregation would ever work for African Americans, he ensured that it would be unsuccessful with a tracking system that labeled (at least as far as the press was concerned) most Black students as intellectually inferior or average. Some of the most powerful studies on tracking over the past three decades have shown that this doubt in desegregated achievement (expressed through ability grouping or tracking) created a self-fulfilling prophecy regarding student achievement and teacher expectations. This has been especially true for people of color.

School districts such as Washington continued to live with their own doubt in their success while creating more and more standardized tests to "track" success. Tracking in this case not only refers to the cataloging of test and percentile scores for students, but also cataloging students themselves as worthy and unworthy, victors and losers. For most Black students, other students of color, and poor students, this tracking is the way politicians, pundits, and the press can justify withholding more educational funds, refusing to provide better trained teachers, and writing these students off as losers in the political game of education.

Regardless of whether there was a "crisis of confidence" or a crisis in education in the D.C. Public Schools, the school board found itself in turmoil after Hansen's resignation in 1967 and remained embroiled in controversy throughout the late-1960s and 1970s. Between 1967 and 1975, D.C. Public Schools had five Superintendents, including two acting ones in 1967 and 1969–70. These Superintendents left their positions primarily because of their inability to eradicate the inertia of the school board and the school board's unwillingness to work with them to solve the problems of the school system. With the advent of school board selection by election and the appointment of Hugh Scott (the first permanent Black school superintendent) in 1969 came a half-decade of difficulties within the District Board of Education and no significant progress on any of the school system's problems. Another *Hobson* decision in 1970 requiring equal spending for each student and the widespread transfer of teachers—along with the first major teacher's strike in Washington's history in the fall of 1972—also helped stall any new initiatives. As these were attacks against a school system in which ninety-four percent of the students, four-fifths of the teachers, six out of 11 board members, and the superintendent were Black, the issues of race and incompetence were obvious in many of the critiques of this period.

In the climate of the late-1960s and early 1970s, a number of District African Americans were also concerned about community involvement with the school system. The Black Power and the Black Studies movements—along with the assassinations of Malcolm X and Martin Luther King—breathed new life into a Black Washington community that had become less active as a result of massive demographic shifts during the 1950s and early 1960s. Activism around a common set of themes was not obvious because so many new Black faces were moving to Washington and because so many changes had occurred in D.C. Public Schools. The radicalizing atmosphere of the period and the rhetorical dismantling of D.C. Public Schools' good reputation by the District newspapers, the *Hobson* decision, and the Passow report invited both new and old Black Washingtonians to rally around a series of issues.

One of the issues that many District African Americans pushed in their work to make D.C. Public Schools a community institution—like they had perceived it before 1954—was to demand the development of a formal curriculum that incorporated the Black experience. In light of the Black Power and Black Studies influence, one could argue that as early as the late-1960s, a number of community organizations and activists were fighting for an Afrocentric curriculum, rather than a multilingual, multicultural one. In reality, African American activists sought the inclusion of African/African American culture as a component of a broader curriculum. From a philosophical perspective, activists eagerly fought for the inclusion of African/African American cultural concepts and histories, but did not necessarily favor a philosophy advocating the denial of the American in the African soul. There is a direct link between the Black Studies/Black Power movements of the late-1960s and Afrocentricity today, but most Black activists in the District were fighting for cultural inclusion, rather than for Afrocentricity (at least as we know it today).

Although D.C. Public Schools had developed curriculum guides on African American history in 1964 and on Black literature in 1968, they were not attached to any substantial changes in the formal curriculum. By the late-1960s, community, student, and local civil rights organizations had mobilized protests, staged school sit-ins and walk-outs, and lobbied the D.C. Board of Education in order to change the climate of failure in the District schools. Local civil rights organizations such as the Black United Front (led by Stokely Carmichael), Associated Community Teams (led by Julius Hobson), the New School of Afro-American Thought, and the Free D.C. Movement (led by soon-to-be school board member and mayor Marion Barry) joined forces and dedicated themselves to improving D.C. Public Schools for Black students. These organizations, in turn, worked with the Washington Teachers Union (WTU) and the Southern Christian Leadership Conference (SCLC), who established the Freedom School as part of the Poor People's Campaign in April 1968. The Freedom School—the educational complement to Martin Luther King's last campaign before his assassination—was created to provide Black youth with a Black Studies program. The New School of Afro-American Thought was another grassroots organization established to provide Black students with an education on the Black experience. The New School's bylaws reflected views of the revolution in Black thought which all the aforementioned organizations shared, as they offered students an "alternative to a 'Black Anglo-Saxon Mentality—' a kind of mental self-determination that may someday bring us self-determination in all other aspects of life."

This statement signifies more than just an attack on mainstream American culture; it captures some Black working-class views of the now old Black elite and the post-1960 middle class. The more common terms that most African Americans use to describe "Black Anglo-Saxons" today are "Oreos" (i.e., Black on the outside, White on the inside) or "Uncle Toms." These organizations emphasized the need for ordinary Blacks to become extraordinary in their struggle to define and redefine the African American identity. This meant abandoning abstract White and elite Black constructions of African America, both of which concerned themselves with producing "respectable Negroes." The contention for these District organizations was that African Americans could only become spiritually and culturally whole human beings through the recognition of their African side and essence.

It should be noted that in the cases of Julius Hobson and Marion Barry, their work in the District during the Civil Rights Movement gave them both the political clout necessary to become two of the first elected D.C. Board of Education members in 1969 and 1971 respectively. Hobson's work during the 1960s to desegregate D.C. Public Schools made him an obvious choice for the District school board, as well as a city council member in 1974. He might well have run for mayor in 1978, except for his death in 1977. Barry, for his part, was a transplanted Washingtonian whose path to power began as a sharecropper's son from rural Mississippi during the Depression decade. After his father's death, Barry, his mother and two sisters moved to Memphis, Tennessee during the 1940s, where he became an excellent student. While working on his doctorate in chemistry at the University of Tennessee—an amazing feat in itself considering Barry's background—Barry's attention turned to the Civil Rights Movement. Along with activists Ella Baker, Julian Bond, and the late Stokely Carmichael (a.k.a., Kwame Ture), Barry helped form the Student Non-Violent Coordinating Committee (SNCC), an offshoot of the SCLC led by Martin Luther King. With the turmoil and chaos that SNCC faced as a result of a loose power structure and gender-based power struggle, Barry was chosen as SNCC's first director in 1965, and moved to Washington to lead their efforts. This work, of course, led to his run for office on the D.C. Board of Education in 1971, for the D.C. City Council in 1974, and for mayor in 1978. And despite his difficulties with drugs and sex, Barry remained mayor from 1978 to 1990 and from 1994–1998. But it was his work and the work of Carmichael, Hobson, and other activists in DC's educational arena that opened up his opportunity to run for office once DC home rule became a reality in 1974.

African American students in D.C. Public Schools also participated in putting pressure on the School Board to create a Black Studies program in the late-1960s. Dunbar High School, Garnet-Patterson Junior High School, and seven other schools staged sit-ins and walk-outs during the 1967–68 and 1968–69 school years. But what was even more significant was the establishment of the Accredited Eastern High Freedom School Annex by students at Eastern High School in Northeast Washington in 1968. These students were running their own Black Studies program apart from their high school, with some help from the WTU and the SCLC. As Eastern High Freedom School teacher Mamadou Lumuma put it, the school's purpose was to help "create love in the community."

These and other activities might have created love, but they also rocked the boat of an already unstable D.C. Board of Education. In the fall of 1969, the D.C. Board of Education, led by Superintendent Hugh Scott and Assistant Superintendent George Rhodes, Jr., approved the implementation of a pilot project coined the Afro-American Experience Program. Over the next five years, five elective classes in African/African American history and literature were introduced to nine of the school district's junior and senior high schools. Swahili classes were also implemented as electives for some of the District's schools during the 1969–70 school year.

But only a separate Black Studies program for all African American students would have sufficed for some Black Washingtonians. The District school board never seriously discussed the development of a full-blown Black Studies program,

and the pilot project was dismantled in 1974. This would not become a significant educational policy issue for D.C. Public School again until the late-1980s.
The same is generally true for urban school districts across the country in this
period. From the teacher's union-defeated independent school district in the
Ocean Hill-Brownsville section of Brooklyn in New York City, to the work of
the Black Panther Party in Chicago and Oakland, California, the push for a more
inclusive curriculum in America's public schools fizzled out as the 1970s pro-
gressed. Within a decade and a half, however, the issue of cultural inclusion
would become prominent again, bringing the culture wars to every major school
district in the country.

All of these activities pressured the D.C. School Board and its superintendents
to seriously examine the issue of curriculum change, specifically in the formal
inclusion of the African American experience. This pressure came with the
already heavy burden of improving student achievement in the District schools.
For the remainder of the century, both issues would be key to the successes and
failures of D.C. Public School superintendents. The question of whether the
issues of curriculum revision and closing the achievement gap were compatible
and could be worked on simultaneously never seemed to come up with the
School Board or the superintendents.

Superintendent Barbara Sizemore was perhaps the most controversial one in
the post-1960s era in the District. One could argue, in fact, that wherever
Sizemore has gone, controversy has followed her. An abrasive personality (something the writer has observed first-hand) combined with turbulent times had cat-
apulted her to great accomplishments while simultaneously wearing out her
welcome. As an administrator with Chicago Public Schools in the late-1960s and
early-1970s, Sizemore directed the Woodlawn Experimental Schools Project,
designed to improve the achievement of African American youth on standardized
tests and in general. Her work in Chicago led directly to her hiring as Superintendent after a national search in 1973. Sizemore's work in D.C. Public Schools during the mid-1970s was influential because it led to major curricula changes after
her departure.

Superintendent Sizemore faced enormous opposition from the divided school
board during her two years in the position. As Sizemore put it, her "superinten-
dency began under a divisive racial cleavage and a distrust of Board leadership."
Among other things, Sizemore attempted to decentralize D.C. Public Schools, to
loosen the control of the school board, and to give District neighborhoods more
power to define the agendas of their schools. Sizemore was building on former
Superintendent Scott's plan of decentralization and community involvement in

order to achieve more community control of the public schools, and to create an atmosphere in which Black student achievement problems could be effectively addressed. She planned to provide curricula that would reflect a "multi-lingual, multi-cultural content emerging from our bilingual programs...changes in the conceptual framework of content organization," and an "emphasis on concepts instead of facts."

The problems that Sizemore and Black Washington faced from the school board in attempting to implement her decentralization plans occurred largely because of political self-interest. Some school board members believed that poor Blacks lacked the knowledge to implement and administer community-based schools. Sizemore saw the school board as two divided factions (whom she called the "Paternalists" and the "Populists"), who were fighting for political crumbs to achieve the best position possible when Washington received home rule in 1974. The "Paternalists" were school board members who believed that elite Blacks should retain centralized control of D.C. Public Schools, while their "Populist" counterparts supported decentralization. All involved assumed that Black Washingtonians would only become politically involved through the efforts of Black leadership because of the community's relative poverty and isolation. Paternalists, though, were distrustful of Populist attempts to mobilize poor District Blacks.

What this produced was a long and bitter stalemate between Superintendent Sizemore and the D.C. Board of Education, which ended in her firing in 1975. Among those who led the charge for Sizemore's removal was Marion Barry, a leader of Sizemore's "Paternalists" and president of the school board. As this was a key political position in post-home rule Washington, an activist such as Barry would use this influence as a stepping stone to the mayor's office. Assisting in the firing of an unpopular school superintendent is certainly one way to garner support in running for mayor. The *Washington Post*, meanwhile, criticized Sizemore and the school board for neglecting educational issues as a result of their bickering, claiming that "both sides have become so engrossed in their reckless and demeaning conflict that they have forfeited any claim to leadership in the city's public schools." Sizemore has continued her work in improving the educational achievement of underprivileged youth and in promoting cultural inclusion since leaving D.C. Public Schools through her positions as a professor of Black Studies at the University of Pittsburgh, Dean of the School of Education at De Paul University in Chicago and currently as a semi-retired professor emerita at De Paul.

The appointment of Vincent Reed as Superintendent of D.C. Public Schools in 1975 brought the first sign of stability that the Board of Education and the school system had experienced since 1954. Reed's pleasant style (at least when compared with Sizemore's) and the fact that he was an insider (Reed had five years' experience in several assistant and associate superintendent positions in the D.C. Public Schools) enabled him to do some of what Sizemore could not. During his administration, Reed gained the trust of the school board and implemented many of Sizemore's suggestions for reform under the Competency-Based Curriculum (CBC) in 1976. Under the CBC, not only were Sizemore's recommendations for outcomes (or criteria) based tests (as opposed to only standardized tests) implemented, but also used national standardized testing norms as the yardstick for measuring a rise or decline in overall student achievement. This curriculum was "built [to be] highly structured...by deciding what it is students need to learn, and by devising criterion-referenced tests to determine whether they had learned." The CBC remained a part of the D.C. Public Schools, with slight modifications, from 1976 to 1997, and had been credited for bringing higher test scores and stability to the school system during the late-1970s and 1980s. When Superintendent Reed resigned in 1980, Superintendent Floretta McKenzie (1981–88) continued his CBC program, and raised standards for coursework and testing. Since the late-1980s, however, overall test scores in D.C. Public Schools have either dropped or remained stagnant. In 1997, a new set of standardized tests were introduced to the schools, with the addition of holding students, teachers, and individual schools accountable for student achievement and student failure.

This should not be too surprising, since at least thirty states from New York to Texas to Illinois have adopted state-required standardized tests which hold students, teachers, and schools accountable for ensuring passing scores in the past four years. The passage of the No Child Left Behind Act in 2002 requires the use of high-stakes testing as the primary accountability measure, meaning that every state must eventually develop a statewide exam. Students who fail these exams will need to repeat their grade level, teachers could lose their jobs, and schools could lose much needed funds. It is the ultimate example of policy makers blaming the victim for educational circumstances they played no role in creating, while at the same time appearing to improve educational standards and expectations.

Since the mid-1980s, part of the focus of D.C. Public Schools has shifted to the issue of Black culture and education, as well as (on at least a theoretical basis) multiculturalism. This was particularly true in the context of Black male-only classrooms. With the decline in student achievement in the late-1980s and other urban school systems considering plans for culturally-inclusive curricula, D.C. Public Schools hopped on the bandwagon. In 1989, a five-year plan was drawn up to develop among other things a multicultural curriculum for the District, while Project 2000 (a program specifically designed for Black male students) was introduced in 1990. Although D.C. Public Schools' official program was to develop both African American-centered and multicultural curricula, almost all of the resources in this cause were thrown into designing classes and curriculum on the African/African American experience. These programs have been delayed in both their development and implementation, as debate over the viability of multiculturalism, Afrocentricity, and Black male-only classrooms continued during the 1990s. D.C. Public Schools did manage to introduce programs that are best described as a mesh of African-centered and multicultural curricula to Webb Elementary School and Spingarn High School in 1993 and 1995 respectively. These programs initially limited the number of students who could participate, but became school-wide once D.C. Public Schools declared Webb and Spingarn semi-independent charter schools in 1996.

Similar to the 1930s, the post-1960 period has been marked by rapid demographic change, serious economic problems, and physical isolation for Black Washington. With a city that has been at least sixty-five percent African American since 1960 and a school system that has been at least ninety percent Black since the mid-1960s, concentrating on the achievements of African ancestors and Africans in America would seem to make sense. After all, hundreds of thousands of Whites left the District for the suburbs, and after 1970, so did large numbers of upper-middle class Blacks. By any standard, D.C. Public Schools has ranked among the worst urban school districts in the United States, with a fifty percent dropout rate, as well as an average student grade point average below a C. There has also been the general sense that teachers (especially White teachers) could care less what happens to these students. Given these set of circumstances and the reality that concentrating on the Black experience is easier to explain than most educators' stupefying notions of multiculturalism, it should not be a surprise that many Black Washingtonians are supportive of efforts that lean toward Afrocentricity.

Black Washington on Education, Race, and the Past, 1960–2000:

Although the school board and D.C. Public School superintendents were not concerned for the most part with issues of curriculum beyond testing, many African American Washingtonians not directly involved with the school system were concerned with more than students exceeding national norms. The legacy of segregation and desegregation, the rise and fall of the Civil Rights and Black Power movements, the many demographic changes to the nature and composition of the District, identity formation, and intraracial relations were among the important issues for Black Washingtonians. As was the case in the 1920s and 1930s, a variety of different perspectives existed among elite, middle, and working-class African Americans on educational and race issues for the post-1960 era.

A number of Black Washingtonians felt that D.C. Public Schools did a better job of training both Black and White students for employment and the realities of the outside world before desegregation. The Black Divisions were also seen as preparing Black students to fight for their civil and human rights while instilling them with race pride. Former D.C. Public Schools teacher and administrator Felicia Chisley said that for "the great masses of [Black] kids, their education began to lessen and…they were not considered like they had been" before desegregation. Nor did she think that "White teachers had a vested interest in our children." This was a specific reference to Chisley's experience as a teacher and counselor in D.C. Public Schools when her White counterparts were forced to teach in integrated (albeit with an ability grouping system in place) situations after 1954. Jeannie Oakes' work as a scholar of educational policy has found that White teachers often have lower expectations of Black students and other students of color than of their White counterparts. Oakes also concluded that lower teacher expectations coincided with the low achieving student groupings those teachers were responsible for. With the majority of America's teachers being White and with most of the low achieving students in urban schools either Black or Brown (and typically poor), low teacher expectations and student achievement have been part of K-12 education's vicious cycle at least since the *Brown* decision.

Chisley also complained about how Black Washingtonians—particularly those in leadership positions—behaved in the wake of desegregation and the Civil Rights Movement of the 1960s. She complained that "a lot of Black people…fled to the suburbs…thinking that their children" would attend an integrated and therefore better school district. Chisley recognized that many elite and middle class Black Washingtonians left the District for the predominantly White suburbs because they believed schools there were better than the formerly segregated school system. Chisley argued that "one of the things that we inherently believed is that if it was White it was right. That was something, that was a fantasy that we had. And we believed that when integration came, everything would be fine…that fantasy has [been] proven wrong." Chisley believed that in the process of fighting for desegregation

> we abdicated responsibility, and we abdicated our strengths…We didn't keep our strengths, we didn't keep our families, we didn't keep our values, see, and

> I believe our values are very different [from Whites]. The values that we had are very different from the values we got with integration. And unfortunately we picked up the worst things.

For Chisley, one of those "worst things" was the American Dream. In maintaining that things are worse now than they were during segregation, she also stated that because Blacks "trusted that people were going to do the right thing, our lives have deteriorated." For Chisley, even though "Black people can have as much money as they want...you can live where you want to...there's still a heavy line between races." This means that elite and middle class Blacks who "don't spend their money doing things that would [not] further other people" have not realized that we "have not arrived."

What Chisley suggested was that Black leaders from the elite class and the new post-1960s Black middle class deluded themselves into believing that the American Dream was achievable when one assimilated into mainstream American society. Chisley was also contending (in an irksome way), and rightly so, that African Americans had bought into an Anglo-American version of the American Dream, which was never meant to include Blacks in the first place. The American Dream can then be perceived as one of predominantly White suburban neighborhoods and schools with equally homogeneous houses, automobiles, dogs, and picket fences. This highly materialistic and allegedly placid vision of a perfect American society falls far short of providing African Americans with the cultural inclusion that many (including Black elites) desired. This was what Chisley saw in the changing face of Black Washington after the 1960s, and part of the dilemma many African Americans face regarding integration today.

Chisley felt that the aging Black elite, even if they had a commitment to the Black Washington community during the 1950s and 1960s, no longer invested their time or money into devising strategies and means for empowerment. Although this is probably an overstatement, it remains that many prominent Blacks are either no longer interested in the larger struggles of African Americans or realize that the work is so overwhelming that they see their efforts as inconsequential. Either way, the leadership that led the charge for desegregation in the District and in American society during the mid-twentieth century had few answers for the post-1960s struggles of everyday Blacks.

Former D.C. Public Schools student and teacher Donna Potts agreed that though de jure segregation was a millstone for Black Washingtonians before 1954, schooling for Blacks in this period had nurtured race pride. Her assessment was that the responsibility for the failures of the post-1960s era "has to be with the Black community because we can't pass anything on, preschool or anything if [we] don't have some pride, some knowledge" of the Black experience. Potts continued: "I've got to have it to give to my child...to be there to give to my child," and "[we] need to reexamine ourselves" regarding race and race pride. Although Potts argued that Blacks "got to have White people in the picture for things to stay equal" when it came to enforcing desegregation and maintaining decent public services (including D.C. Public Schools), she also urged "for [Blacks] to learn and...to get ahead and...be the best people we can be...I don't have to be in the room with [Whites]." Potts, like Chisley, had taught in D.C. Public Schools during the late-1960s and 1970s, in the midst of the Black Power and Black Studies movements, as well as during the Board of Education and Superintendent turmoil. Her views have a tone that reflects these post-1960 influences, in addition to her experiences growing up in the District in the 1950s and 1960s.

Old Black elites did not see the pre-1954 days as ones that contained any redeeming qualities. They saw the desegregation process and the Civil Rights Movement during the 1950s and 1960s as watershed events leading to first-class citizenship. A 1980 *Washington Post* article written by current ABC News correspondent Michel Martin (formerly Michel McQueen) illuminated the thoughts of Dunbar High's Class of 1935 in which a number of elite Black Washingtonians voiced their opinions about desegregation and about non-elite Blacks who did not wholeheartedly believe in the strategy. Mary Huntley, a teacher at the formerly elite Dunbar High School during the mid-twentieth century and author of *The Dunbar Story* (1965), remarked that "it's the cotton pickers running the city who are jealous of what we have accomplished here." She added that "you've got to look like a cotton picker and speak Black English to get listened to, but we live in an integrated country and people preaching segregation are closing the door in their own face."

Certainly Huntley was describing Marion Barry, the son of a Mississippi sharecropper who had ascended to the Mayor's office in 1978. Huntley, unfortunately, was also spewing her views of many Black Washingtonians, particularly those who had migrated into the area from the Deep South after World War II. For her and for many of her elite brothers and sisters, the wave of Black migration into the District between 1945 and 1970 brought "cotton pickers" such as Marion Barry, who were sending the city to hell in a hand basket. Power struggles in the city government and the school board, along with attempts to Africanize the school district's curriculum obviously did not sit well with Huntley. She believed that the battle over equal educational opportunities had mostly been won during the 1950s and 1960s. Although it was apparent that the desegregation pill did not cure the racial and economic inequality disease—and caused side effects such as self-absorbing nostalgia—Huntley remained a blind adherent to the power of desegregation to give Blacks a chance at the American Dream. Huntley's perspective also highlights the fear and apprehension of many old elites to the post-home rule Washington. The city was now a place where everyday African Americans could vote for cotton-pickers such as Barry, could vote for school board members who revamped Dunbar into a non-elite high school or might change the curriculum, and could make the role of the remaining Black elite in Washington perfunctory. Huntley's fear was one of falling status, and her views in the *Post* article confirm that fact.

Members of this particular group of elite Black Washingtonians apparently looked forward to desegregation during the 1950s. Charlotte Brooks, a Class of 1935 graduate, argued that while "we didn't just close up and die because the White world excluded us" before 1954, "when integration came we were ready." Marvin Hightower supported integration for more selfish reasons, as it allowed him to "go for the gusto" in building his own business. According to Hightower, "[e]verything I did, I did for me, and that's the way you should go."

For Huntley, Brooks, and especially Hightower, desegregation meant the ability to operate as individuals who achieved because of hard work; the issue of race became irrelevant. Their statements in some ways confirm the views of non-elite Black Washingtonians like Chisley and Potts, who believed that elite Blacks had bought into mainstream American values such as individualism, the Protestant work ethic, and conspicuous consumption. At the same time, this group of elite African Americans discarded the mantle of race uplift as a part of their life's work and their rhetoric, which was a major shift from the previous generation of elites. Their views also reflected what desegregation had become since the 1930s; a simple process by which many well-positioned Blacks and a few extremely gifted non-elite Blacks could advance in American society without advancing the race. While this is progress, it hardly represents the progress desired by desegregation advocates such as Mary Church Terrell, Kelly Miller, and the late Thurgood Marshall.

Unlike the Dunbar graduates of the Class of 1935, and like Chisley and Potts, Black Washingtonian resident Edward Feggans saw the immediate post-1954 period as one in which the community deteriorated, in part because elite Blacks were ready to "go for the gusto" of desegregation. From Feggans' perspective, serious problems developed as the post-World War II prosperity reached African Americans and as the Supreme Court declared segregation unconstitutional. As "we were able to afford the better clubs and hotels open[ed] to us" downtown, according to Feggans, "it just left no room for a Black businessman to have a club...when you could go downtown and see a good show." Feggans insisted that patronizing "anything but something Black, you know...is a negative part of our heritage that we are not mad" about because many African Americans, particularly the elite, preferred White businesses and services in downtown Washington. As was the case with Chisley, Feggans felt that prominent Blacks could not wait to flock to White businesses because they assumed that anything "White" was automatically better than anything "Black." The fact that some elite Blacks refused to build businesses and support Black establishments as part of their overall strategy for race uplift—along with their abandonment of Black Washington for the suburbs—led Feggans to conclude that the old Black elite and the post-1960s Black middle class were both "complacent" and "apathetic."

Problems such as intrarace relations and defining the right strategy for Black empowerment in Washington persisted even after the emergence of a post-*Brown* and post-Civil Rights era Black elite and middle class. Where the old Black elite continue to bask in the glory of their achievements, non-elite Blacks from the mid-twentieth century saw those achievements as short-sighted and selfish. The connection that some African Americans made between economic problems and the attitudes of the old Black elite and new Black middle class in fact led them to conclude that desegregation was a failed strategy. It was a failure not only because it did not permanently desegregate D.C. Public Schools and the District beyond legal definitions. It also failed because the cultural and economic concerns of many non-elite African Americans went unconsidered in the process.

These activities and perspectives represent post-1960 formulations of multiculturalism and Afrocentricity. They also show that desegregation had thoroughly failed Black Washington. Resegregation due to "White flight," the exodus of the old Black elite and upper-middle class Black to the suburbs, and the continued movement of large numbers of African Americans to the city helped make the schools more than ninety percent Black and significantly poorer by the 1960s. Problems of student achievement, negative press coverage, two *Hobson v. Hansen* decisions, and monumental reports on the horrors of the District schools left it with nearly a decade and a half of political turmoil. This chaos has yet to be fully resolved, even with the advent of home rule in Washington in 1974. In the last decade, there have also been attempts to implement multicultural and Afrocentric curricula in the public schools. Yet, poor overall student achievement, fiscal problems, and school board friction remain a part of D.C. Public Schools' challenge for the twenty-first century.

Washington African Americans, despite the *Brown* decision, the Civil Rights Movement, and the blurring of the intrarace class and color lines that have occurred since the 1930s, also face serious fissures from within. The post-1960 problems of D.C. Public Schools are a microcosm of the issues that face the Black Washington community. Even with home rule, prominent Blacks and ordinary African Americans still disagree on the purpose and legacy of desegregation, the sincerity of Black leaders holding positions of power, and on the future direction of African American energies in Washington. While ordinary Black Washingtonians question the sincerity of their elite and new upper-middle class comrades because of their "flight" to the Virginia and Maryland suburbs, elites attack formerly rank-and-file Blacks because of their alleged "cotton-picking" mentality. Despite their disagreements, African Americans regardless of class and color in the District continue to see education as a major player in their future, with a number suggesting that multiculturalism in the schools and in the community is imperative to this process. Far more Blacks, however, seem to be most supportive of curriculum reforms that can only be described as Afrocentric. In any case, many District Blacks persist in their belief that if their children are trained to succeed in both Black and mainstream America, then they can help uplift the race individually and collectively.

The more recent studies of D.C. Public Schools and the post-1960 Black Washington community also suggest that the development of multiculturalism and Afrocentricity accelerated with the realization in the 1960s that desegregation was not the panacea for African American problems. It had not even solved the problems of education for prominent Black Washingtonians. For lower middle class, working-class, and poor Blacks in Washington, the problems of education, poverty, and crime worsened. Resegregation isolated these groups from suburban Whites along with suburban upper middle class and elite Blacks in the specific context of schooling.

All of these changes point to the fear of the future for both elite and ordinary African Americans. This would explain the nostalgia of many old Black Washingtonian elites for the glory days of desegregation, as well as the yearning of everyday African Americans for the difficult yet more cohesive days of segregation. With Washington's depressing times regarding D.C. Public Schools, the city governance, and increasing poverty, is there any wonder why many older Black Washingtonians fear the future and wax nostalgic about the more hopeful past? In his *I May Not Get There With You* (2000), Michael Eric Dyson categorizes the nostalgia of Americans (Black and White) when contemplating Martin Luther

King and the Civil Rights era as "cultural amnesia," a fairly apt term for also describing Black Washingtonian views of the state of their community.

In spite of these conditions, the District Black community remained active in pressuring the D.C. Public Schools to respond to their demands for academic excellence and curriculum reform. This might be surprising to some because so many prominent and upper middle class African Americans have left for the suburbs, taking their money and activism with them. As Mary Patillo-McCoy has recently noted for Chicago in her book *Black Picket Fences* (1999), large numbers of lower and solidly middle class African Americans have remained in predominantly Black inner city communities because of the persistence of residential segregation. In the greater Washington area, there is a high financial price to pay if one intends to move to the suburbs, higher in some respects than remaining in one of most expensive cities in the United States. Family and cultural ties are among other reasons those who are on the fringes of leaving for suburban Washington have remained in the District, despite diminishing services. At the same time, activism from lower middle class and poor African Americans on issues such as the expansion of Metro (the DC-area subway system) service in their communities and the development of Afrocentric and multicultural curricula for D.C. Public Schools has kept a bad set of circumstances from worsening.

It is not necessarily important for the activism of District African Americans to be channeled more toward multiculturalism than Afrocentricity. This is partly because many Black Washingtonians view the D.C. Public Schools as part of a larger society which has attempted to isolate them and make their lives irrelevant. In other words, their embracing of education that is African/African American-centered is in part a response to decades of cultural exclusion, economic stagnation, and societal scapegoating. Plus, a curriculum that concentrates on African heritage and the Black experience in America is not automatically bad, so long as there is some recognition that the raising of self-esteem and educational excellence are different subjects. The topics are related, but not as directly as some advocates might believe. Certainly some District African Americans realize that schools must continue to promote an understanding of American society as a whole if one expects Black students with pride in their heritage to succeed educationally and otherwise.

All too often, unfortunately, educators, scholars, policy makers, and other experts make the assumption that what ordinary African Americans in the District and in general want in terms of curriculum reform is exactly what experts in Afrocentricity want. This of course generates fear and loathing between experts who believe in the status quo of an Anglo-centered education and experts who believe in nothing but Afrocentricity for Black students. Ordinary African Americans, in turn, have become more passionate in their support for Afrocentricity. The problem with so many of these so-called experts and their ideas is also the other part of the reason why support for Afrocentricity is not necessarily bad: no one really knows how either multiculturalism or Afrocentricity works as practical concepts or curricula. Those who are true believers in Afrocentricity on closer examination may very well be supporters of multiculturalism, and those who believe in multiculturalism could also be advocates for Afrocentricity. Without clear-cut definitions that differentiate the two concepts, experts and laypersons who would normally be in agreement with each other instead can find themselves on opposite sides of this issue.

What can also happen as a result of this confusion is that prominent scholars and policy makers can deliberately link one to the other. They can argue that multiculturalism is bad because Afrocentricity is bad and say that multiculturalism and Afrocentricity are one and the same without most experts and laymen understanding that there are differences. And the confusion over multiculturalism and Afrocentricity can limit the ability of groups such as District African Americans to push for curriculum change because they and the school district might not know exactly *what* the curriculum is being transformed into. This might explain why African Americans and other people of color—who probably have the most to gain from multiculturalism—have shown little interest in the concept despite the recent "culture wars."

Part Three: Multiculturalism's Multiple Misdiagnoses

5

The Ultimate Fear Realized: Public Policy, Multiculturalism and Race in the 1990s

In a conversation with a friend several years ago, we concluded that even in the loftiest of circles that groups such as African Americans are treated as if they were a Black box. The idea here is that many scholars, pundits, policy makers, and politicians address people of color and their issues by studying them from afar. In the case of African Americans and other people of color, the Black box analogy is appropriate because the problem of acknowledging and understanding these groups is not a matter of physical distance. It is instead a matter of long-standing assumptions and fear of the unknown, including the loss of status.

For example, many "experts" can tell the American public the African American community—in this case, the Black box—is Black with six sides, square, and made of wood. This tells us nothing about what the box's contents are, including its compartments, residents, and other unique features. Similarly, many talking heads can speak of African Americans—who comprise roughly thirteen percent of the American population—by mentioning that in most social, economic, and educational indicators, Blacks have closed the gap but still lag behind Whites, with many Blacks living in crime-ridden, poverty-stricken, urban central cities, and that they were once an enslaved people. These general descriptors are problematic because they lack the depth needed to acknowledge and understand the unique features of Black America, including issues of family, gender, history, and education, along with the more stereotypical examinations of music, religion and athletics. But like a Black box, "experts" are uneasy about opening up the Black community for a full examination of its contents.

A major theme in Robin D. G. Kelley's *Yo' Mama's Disfunktional!* (1997) involves dispelling the myth of a monolithic Black urban culture perpetuated by social science research. Kelley objects to social science generalizations that depict urban Black culture "as a static, measurable thing—behavior" in the aptly titled chapter "Looking for the 'Real' Nigga." Kelley stresses that "[b]y conceiving Black urban culture in the singular," scholars merely depict African Americans as "cardboard typologies who fit neatly into their own definition of the 'underclass' and render invisible" African America in all of its cultural complexity. Included within this complexity are "aesthetics, style, and visceral pleasures," as well as "Black urban culture's multicultural roots." Most "experts," unfortunately, have yet to realize the radical idea that in order to understand urban African America's "multicultural roots," they first must open the supposedly scary "Black box" and view what is inside.

This chapter examines why so many so-called experts are afraid of multicultur-alism and deep considerations of people of color. It is a catalog of how educators have attempted to introduce this philosophy to American education and the neg-ative responses to multiculturalism by America's cultural gatekeepers. The main alleged experts discussed here include Arthur Schlesinger, Jr., William Bennett, Dinesh D'Souza, and Diane Ravitch. One key element to answering the question of why there is so much fear of multiculturalism is how these gatekeepers have deliberately or inadvertently confused multiculturalism with Afrocentricity, which means that part of the fear of multiculturalism is a fear of Black America. At the same time, the chapter addresses the writings of some advocates of multi-culturalism among the experts, finding that some of their propositions have added fuel to the arguments of those who are against multiculturalism. Because of the controversy over multiculturalism (and indirectly, race) in the past decade, those probably best able to help introduce multiculturalism to American educa-tion—namely African Americans and other people of color—have been excluded from this process.

Multiculturalism and Afrocentricity in Educational Policy, 1964–85:

Multiculturalism as we seem to understand it today developed from the series of cultural movements that themselves evolved from the Civil Rights Movement of the 1960s. Included among these were the Black Studies, Chicano, Women's, American Indian, and Gay Rights movements. Activists demanded the inclusion of their experiences in college and university-level curricula throughout the 1960s and 1970s. Scholars of multicultural education became prominent during the 1970s, including James Banks, Christine Sleeter, and Carl Grant. These move-ments and scholars had succeeded by the early 1980s in establishing Black, Women's, Chicano, and other identity studies programs at a majority of Amer-ica's colleges and universities.

Advocates for a multicultural perspective in education then shifted their focus to K-12 education. Their argument—similar to what it had been for Black Washingtonians in the 1920s and 1930s—was that K-12 education had excluded people of color and women (not to mention non-elites in general) from the curriculum and textbooks while also teaching these groups about great, dead, rich WASP men. Parents, teachers, scholars, and other advocates voiced their concerns. Combined with more scholarship on multiculturalism in education, community activists influenced school boards to examine the prospect of adopting multicultural curricula.

The first major school district to formally implement a multicultural curriculum was Portland, Oregon in 1985. The district developed this curriculum as part of their 1982 desegregation plan to not only physically integrate their schools, but to also make them culturally inclusive. They employed a number of scholars (most notably Asa Hilliard) as consultants for developing the *Portland Baseline Essays* for the school district. These essays not only provided historical and cultural background for all major American ethnic/racial groups (African, Asian, Latino, European, and Native Americans). They went beyond historical and cultural generalities by describing the social and economic changes various groups experienced over time. The Portland essays also addressed issues involving gender and religious diversity.

The district designed a curriculum use in Social Studies, English, Math, and Science classes (the last two with the hope that this would enable teachers to relate to their students). It is ironic that the first major urban school district to adopt such a broad program would be Portland, considering that its school district was seventy-five percent White at the time. Note, too, Portland's school district demographics in 1985 were representative of the United States as a whole, if divided strictly by White and persons of colors.

Afrocentricity had picked up steam as a viable alternative to both multiculturalism and the Anglo-centered curriculum during the 1980s with the rise to national and controversial prominence of Molefi Asante (the so-called "Father" of Afrocentricity), Maulana Karenga (one of the founders of the Black Studies movement), Leonard Jeffries, and Francis Cress Welsing. Welsing, by the way, is best known for her book *The Isis Papers* (1991), which promotes what is known in Afrocentric circles as "melanin theory." She argued that melanin (the chemical that produces Brown skin) essentially makes people of color, and specifically those of African descent, physically, spiritually, and intellectually superior to Whites. Some Afrocentrists use melanin to explain the rise of African and Asian civilizations in ancient times, as well as the need for the Greeks to copy Egyptian civilization.

During the 1980s Karenga published a series of textbooks on Black Studies, with the common theme of combating Eurocentric oppression through an African American emphasis of their Africanness. This meant that African Americans should focus on pre-Columbian African cultures, histories, religious practices, ceremonies, and clothing. This was more than just wearing dashikis and kente cloth. Karenga had developed what he coined the Kawaida Principles, a series of statements about traditional African practices of unity, peace, and harmony with nature. Karenga also helped develop Kwanzaa, a celebration to replace Christmas for African Americans, as Christmas supposedly celebrates a "White" God. Kwanzaa is simply a collage of ideas based on traditional African religious practices that give libations and offerings to ancestral spirits for prosperity and success. Both became popular among African Americans during the 1980s.

The prime mover in the rise of Afrocentricity since the early-1980s has been Molefi Asante. His books *Afrocentricity* (1980) and *The Afrocentric Idea* (1987) are Asante's vision that all things ancient and African would provide African Americans with a true identity for themselves and build self-esteem. Asante also proclaimed that Egypt rather than Greece was where Western civilization originated, and that "the preponderant Eurocentric myths of universalism, objectivity, and classical traditions retain a provincial European cast." For Asante, scholarship "rooted in such a tradition obviously lacks either historical or conceptual authority." To put this another way, Asante concluded that the Western belief in a Western civilization created by the West, maintained by the West, and perfected by the West without any outside (specifically African/Egyptian) influence is simply a bald-faced lie. Combined with Martin Bernal's two-volume series *Black Athena* (1987, 1991) on the African origins of Western civilization, Afrocentricity became for most White scholars a philosophy that promoted false history.

The blanket denouncement of Afrocentricity in White circles strengthened Black support for the philosophy, primarily because the rules of race in America dictate that any Black under constant attack from Whites must be doing something good for Blacks. Like Marcus Garvey, Malcolm X, and Louis Farrakhan (although Asante is probably not in their class), Asante's work promotes the idea that African Americans possess a great heritage of building civilizations and that if they can access that heritage, they can then reclaim their rightful place in the world. As Michael Eric Dyson points out in *Race Rules* (1996), attacks by White Americans on Black leaders of any kind pushes African Americans toward those leaders and their ideas rather than away from them precisely because of the history of race in America. A "bad ass Black man" like Asante and his Afrocentric idea(s) would have appeal even without White criticism, but he and Afrocentricity have much more legitimacy among African Americans as a result of it.

Unfortunately for African Americans who supported multiculturalism in education, the voices promoting Afrocentricity were louder and gained more media attention. Because multiculturalism*does not* purport that African culture(s) are the sole origin of Western civilization—and because multicultural educators such as Banks, Sleeter, and Grant do not seek media attention (it's not what academics typically do)—Afrocentricity has become a gigantic lightning rod for the issue of curriculum reform. The advent of Afrocentricity also made it easier for multiculturalism to be struck by the lightning of conservatism in educational politics and burned by association.

By labeling all things African American Afrocentricity, critics obscure the variety of other voices on multiculturalism specifically and on educational reform more generally. Afrocentricity's promoters and critics have even muted the other alternative voices on Afrocentricity. In his book *Afrotopia* (1998), Wilson J. Moses denounced Asante and his recipe for Afrocentricity as "Egyptocentrism," which is "the sometimes sentimental, at other times cynical, attempt to claim ancient Egyptian ancestry for Black Americans. It involves the attempt to reconstruct the peoples of ancient Egypt in terms of traditional American racial perceptions." Moses realized that his examination of the historical relationship between Black cultural traditions and popular culture would "offend both the advocates and the opponents of sentimental Afrocentrism and romantic Egyptocentrism" because of his argument "that they are usually harmless and inoffensive, if sometimes extravagant, folk traditions."

Despite Moses' interesting analysis, Asante can call himself and is considered "the Father of Afrocentricity" because he has regularly availed himself to the media about the philosophy. In America's current climate, educational policy and politics are oftentimes played out in the press, not just in the scholarly community, and not just in school committee meetings. This fact is also the reason that so many ordinary African Americans and other people of color—not to mention Americans in general—are excluded from the process of curriculum and educational reform. The press typically looks for and finds controversy, and is generally not interested in what average citizens have to say about multiculturalism, Afrocentricity, and curriculum reform. The press (and White America more generally) also looks for African Americans who represent the one or two viewpoints that fit within their own preconceived notions of Black thought. Flashy Afrocentrists and prominent conservatives, as far as the media are concerned, establish educational policy, not everyday African Americans, not the average American citizen, and not multicultural scholars in their secluded ivory towers.

Educational Policy Makers and Multiculturalism, 1985–Present:

Other major school districts, impressed by Portland's example, followed in introducing multicultural programs between 1985 and 1991. Included among those districts were Milwaukee, Atlanta, and Washington, D.C. There were two fundamental differences in the implementation scenario in Portland versus the ones in the other cities. For one, Milwaukee, Atlanta, and Washington all had school districts in which Blacks made up at least ninety percent of the student enrollment. This basic demographic fact led to the determination by all three school districts to phase in a multicultural curriculum, starting with the African American experience. This was the second major difference from the Portland example, as the African American curriculum became the central focal point of curriculum change in Milwaukee, Atlanta, and Washington between 1985 and 1991.

Conservative educators, policy makers, and politicians, already unhappy with similar developments in higher education, became more vocal in their opposition to multiculturalism and what they saw as "identity politics." The implementation methods used in Milwaukee, Atlanta, and Washington did not help matters, as their African American curricula seemed to move toward an Afrocentric perspective by the end of the 1980s. Examples of this include Kwanzaa celebrations, the use of African-centered texts written by Karenga and Asante, and the initial talk of developing separate African American male classrooms/schools. The resurgence of Malcolm X as a Black cultural icon heightened conservative fears of a multicultural (read "African American") curriculum. As far as former Secretary of Education and Drug Czar William J. Bennett was concerned, only "traditional education policies" would be successful in achieving the goal of successfully teaching diverse groups of students. For Bennett, "selecting works" and programs "based on the ethnicity or gender of their authors trivializes the academic enterprise."

New York State and Multiculturalism:

The media and the academy began to examine multiculturalism in the public schools more closely in the spring of 1991 as New York State attempted for the second time in three years to develop a multicultural curriculum for K-12 social studies/history. The New York State Department of Education in July 1990 appointed a wide range of scholars and educators—among them Asa Hilliard, Leonard Jeffries (an outside consultant), Nathan Glazer, and Arthur Schlesinger,

Jr.,—to serve on a task force that would develop this curriculum. The New York State Social Studies Review and Development Committee was the formal name of the task force.

By the spring of 1991, the bickering between these scholars and educators had become regular fodder for the *New York Times* and the *Wall Street Journal,* as critics labeled the multicultural curriculum "Afrocentric." Hilliard, Jeffries, Glazer, and Schlesinger did most of the bickering (in the board room as well as in the press), with Jeffries, Hilliard, and other committee members wanting to make more changes to the existing curriculum, and with Glazer and Schlesinger wanting few (if any) changes. Some went so far as to argue for a separate Afrocentric curriculum, while Schlesinger claimed he did not see the point of making any changes at all. In particular, Jeffries and Hilliard believed that the new curriculum should pay more attention to the African origins of Western civilization and African cultures prior to the "Age of Exploration." Schlesinger thought it was silly to spend time in the new curriculum suggesting that the phrase "enslaved persons" was better to use when referring to Africans in bondage than the word slaves. He also added that the report was "saturated with *pluribus* and neglectful of *unum.*"

The media picked up on this acidic debate in May and June 1991, labeling the multicultural curriculum Afrocentric and Hilliard and Jeffries as radicals. By the end of June, several major newspapers had run articles on the rise of the Afrocentric curriculum in America's public schools and its advocation by militant Black scholars and educators. Lost in all the sensationalism was the finalization of the New York State Social Studies Review and Development Committee report for developing a multicultural social studies curriculum in June 1991. *One Nation, Many Peoples: A Declaration of Cultural Interdependence* came off the printing press, and its actual contents barely made a controversial ripple in the media.

The report was careful in labeling the curriculum multicultural, with sections devoted to African, Hispanic, Asian, and Native American experiences in conjunction with mainstream American history. The report also created curriculum categories that concentrated on gender, religious, immigrant, and class issues. Additionally, *One Nation, Many Peoples* had a section that examined world history and its relationship to America's multiple cultures. Despite all of these laudable recommendations, critics nevertheless blasted the report as Afrocentric mythology. In the end, New York State adopted portions of the report's recommendations by 1994, and other parts of the report became a part of the newly implemented Global History curriculum that the state introduced in September 1999.

The New York State controversy sparked a renewed interest among educational policy makers and scholars to discredit multiculturalism as the opposite of *e pluribus unum* ("out of many one"). In the four years before the New York State issue touched already raw nerves, a number of authors had attacked multiculturalism as a threat to academic freedom and the free speech of students at colleges and universities. From Allan Bloom's *The Closing of the American Mind* (the number one best-selling non-fiction book of 1987) to Dinesh D'Souza's *Illiberal Education* (1991), the reason for wanting multiculturalism off college campuses was the same: that White males who spoke English built American society. Bloom argued that American colleges and universities, as well as American society as a whole, are responsible for the closing of the American mind because they contain no core set of traditional Western values. This "openness" to a diversity of ideas and people allows Americans to "not need others. Thus what is advertised as a great opening is a great closing." Bloom believed that multiculturalism would destroy American higher education and American culture because of its polarizing "openness."

D'Souza declared that multicultural programs did damage to the college curriculum because they reflected "a new cultural imperialism no less narrow and bigoted than that of the colonialist researchers in safari outfits and pith helmets." This, of course, was a not-so-subtle reference to Africa on D'Souza's part and what would become an all-too-common theme when criticizing multiculturalism—call it Afrocentrism to exacerbate conservative fears specifically and White American ones more generally. Diane Ravitch, a leading educational policy maker and an educational advisor to the Reagan and Bush administrations, alleged that multiculturalism was "particularistic" and "e pluribus plures" (out of the many, many more) instead of e pluribus unum.

So in the aftermath of the Great Debate of 1991, a whole new set of monographs on the perils of multiculturalism in America's public schools reached the printing presses, including ones by Arthur Schlesinger, Jr. and the former Secretary of Education and Drug Czar (under the Reagan and Bush administrations respectively) William Bennett. Bennett, who certainly is better known for his 1998 treatise denouncing the Bill Clinton's of America (*The Death of Outrage*), jumped into the multiculturalism debate with both feet in 1992. As the title *The De-Valuing of America: The Fight for Our Culture and Our Children* indicates, Bennett believed that "fads" such as multiculturalism were "poison" to America's common culture. Bennett argued that while "[n]ot all efforts at introducing a multicultural curriculum in our schools are bad...for many other advocates of a multicultural—or more precisely, 'Afrocentric'—curriculum, the purpose is the politicization of the curriculum, the promulgation of cultural myths, the distortion of American history, and the primacy of ethnic and racial thinking (the 'new tribalism' as it's been called)."

Bennett concluded that multiculturalism (or Afrocentricity) would "divorce Blacks completely from the mainstream of American life and increase the alienation that many Blacks feel toward the rest of our society and our central civic institutions." Bennett's rants against multiculturalism via Afrocentricity ring hollow with this statement:

> Our common culture serves as a kind of immunological system, destroying the values and attitudes promulgated by an adversary culture that can infect our body politic. Should our common culture begin to break down, should its fundamental premises fail to be transmitted to succeeding generations, then we will have reason to worry. One vital instrument for the transmission of the common culture is our educational system, and we need to ensure that our schools meet that responsibility.

Certainly Bennett's description of America is arrogant in that he attempted to proclaim that an Anglo-dominated culture and "our common culture" are one and the same. But there is more to Bennett's statement than that. He was also suggesting that those forces fighting for Afrocentricity—allegedly in the guise of multiculturalism—and those who would be its consumers (African Americans) are fighting a war against American society. Those in favor of the status quo ("our common culture") represent "us," whereas those supporters of multiculturalism (or Afrocentricity) represent "them."

Schlesinger's *Disuniting of America* presented a similar tale, with the 1991 New York State controversy as the backdrop for his reasoning that multiculturalism was dangerous to the American fabric. Schlesinger, however, took a step that even Bennett had not, which was to presume that he knew what African Americans thought about multiculturalism or Afrocentricity, ethnocentrism, and the "cult of ethnicity." Schlesinger contended that "few Black Americans have regarded the African connection as a major theme in their lives" until the advent of Afrocentricity in the 1980s. Among Schlesinger's examples of Black American disinterest in Africa were a series of quotes from W. E. B. Du Bois's *Dusk of Dawn* (1940) autobiography, in which Du Bois noted that neither his "father nor [his] father's father ever saw Africa or knew its meaning or cared overmuch for it." Schlesinger continued his quotation-out-of-context diatribe regarding Du Bois in supporting his vision of an Anglo-centered American culture, as Du Bois declared:

> Once for all, let us realize that we are Americans, that we were brought here with the earliest settlers and that the very sort of civilization from which we came made the complete absorption of Western modes and customs imperative if we were to survive at all; in brief, there is nothing so indigenous, so completely 'made in America' as we."

Although Schlesinger briefly (and grudgingly) considered that "Du Bois himself spent his last years in West Africa," he then claimed that "Du Bois had earlier dismissed the African connection" to the African American identity.

Du Bois, in contrast, argued that between 1910 and 1930, he had "emerged with a program of Pan-Africanism, as organized protection of the Negro world led by American Negroes" and "was a main factor" in making "Negroes aware of themselves, confident of their possibilities and determined in self-assertion." Despite Schlesinger's best efforts, it appears that Du Bois—among other Black intellectuals—was interested in an African American identity based at least in part on the idea of an African essence, rather than solely on the assimilation of Anglo-American ideals. These ideas came from a combination of experience and educational training, which Schlesinger and other assimilationists refused to consider in their attacks on multiculturalism and similar notions.

These incredibly flawed yet appealing arguments did three things in educational policy and public discourse circles. One, it helped confuse the American public about multiculturalism and Afrocentricity, making two very different concepts exactly the same. This in turn made it far more difficult for states and school districts to adopt any multicultural curriculum, as this issue in educational policy was now toxically charged with the filth of politics. And third, it isolated voices from the African American community, as policy makers and the American public would regard their demands for the Black experience in the K-12 curriculum (whether through multiculturalism or Afrocentricity) as a direct attack on America's homogeneous White culture.

New York City and the Rainbow Curriculum:

The case of the New York City Public School's "Rainbow Curriculum" for elementary school students highlights how poisonous the debates over multiculturalism had become once the so-called experts had condemned it. In the 1989–90 school year, the New York City Board of Education—led by the then popular Chancellor Joseph Fernandez—assembled a committee of educators and teachers to construct a K-6 level multicultural curriculum. Over the next two years, the committee did just that without much publicity and surprisingly little controversy, releasing their 443-page "Children of the Rainbow" (more infamously known as the "Rainbow Curriculum") report and curriculum in the fall of 1991. The committee decided to make the curriculum as all-inclusive as possible, covering all the major ethnic groups, as well as religion, gender, and even class.

They somehow did not anticipate that covering sexual orientation would be controversial. Several members of New York City's local school boards—especially District 24 in Queens and its board president, Mary A. Cummins—were incensed over any mention of sexual orientation in the report. They were particularly upset over the recommendation that the book *Heather Has Two Mommies*—a children's book written to explain a loving relationship between two women—should be used in the classroom. Cummings and others saw the passages on sexual orientation as simply "part of the homosexual movement. It was gay and lesbian propaganda." She also accused Fernandez of perpetrating "as big a lie as any concocted by Hitler or Stalin." After Cummins and District 24 refused to implement the "Rainbow Curriculum" under any circumstances, Chancellor Fernandez suspended the local board on December 1, 1992.

Although the New York City Board of Education had nullified Fernandez's suspension order by December 10, his action had the unfortunate result of greatly intensifying the media coverage of the controversy. Between December 1992 and March 1993, the New York newspapers regularly published articles about the controversial curriculum, giving a voice to Cummins and her supporters regarding the "Rainbow Curriculum" and their belief that it would promote sodomy. Chancellor Fernandez responded that Cummins and the anti-"Rainbow Curriculum" opposition were leading a "malicious, highly organized campaign to distort" the contents of the curriculum for all New Yorkers. The *New York Times* noted that "some blame for misconceptions lies with television and newspapers, which sensationalized the issue or condensed it into headlines that most often included the word 'gay,' leaving an impression that the curriculum talked about nothing else."

It was clear that opponents to the new curriculum and to multiculturalism in general had found an issue that crossed ethnic and racial lines, as most New Yorkers (White, Black, and Hispanic) wanted the rainbow out of the "Rainbow Curriculum." Many New Yorkers, in fact, wanted the "Rainbow Curriculum" eliminated entirely and Fernandez fired for stirring up so much trouble. The Reverend Ruben Diaz of the Bronx Hispanic Clergy Organization, in speaking for (as if any one person could) the New York Hispanic community said "We don't want him. We want him to go back to Miami."

At the end of January 1993, Chancellor Fernandez gave in to some of his opponents demands by deleting *Heather Has Two Mommies* from the report and authorizing a wording change in the report. The terms "gay" and "lesbian" would now be replaced with the allegedly less offensive phrase "same gender." The primary reason Fernandez attempted to offer an olive branch was because he faced an ultimatum. The Board of Education had told Fernandez that they would have to make a decision to either renew his contract (which would expire on June 30, 1993) or allow him leave to his post after February. Despite Fernandez's efforts at reconciliation and compromise, the Board of Education decided in early March not to renew his contract, in effect firing Fernandez. All of this was the result of a three-page section on sexual orientation in a nearly 500-page report that concentrated more heavily on ethnicity and culture than on anything else. The "Rainbow Curriculum," in the end, died because of exposure to the ultraviolet radiation of educational politics. It also died because by 1993, opponents of multiculturalism had done a really good job of making it into Afrocentricity and gay propaganda, the equivalent of a 1990s cultural Antichrist.

National History Standards:

As the controversy over multiculturalism approached an uneasy stalemate (in which no other major school districts adopted it while others with it did not expand it), a new debate broke out over the National History Standards (NHS). In October 1994, the National Council for History Standards released a series of reports with corresponding curriculum materials to the public. The group, led by American social historian Gary Nash and educator Charlotte Crabtree, was really a conglomerate of extremely interested parties, with money and endorsements from the U.S. Department of Education, the National Endowment for the Humanities (NEH), the Organization of American Historians (OAH), and the National Education Association (NEA). The NEH and the Department of Education charged the National Council with the duty of taking K-12 social studies/ history beyond the dark ages of date memorization and name regurgitation (especially of dead WASP males). The organization expected the NHS to incorporate cutting-edge historical analysis based on the experiences of ordinary Whites, peoples of color, and elite WASP males. What social historians have called "bottom-up" history or the "history of the masses" since the 1960s finally was being assembled for K-12 students. Nash, who was a major player in the development of social history during the 1970s and 1980s, was initially enthusiastic about the results of the project. Both Nash and Crabtree believed that the NHS marked "the first milestone in the development of standards of excellence for the nation's public schools."

All of this began to change even before the release of the NHS. In October 1994, the 700 Club and the Christian Broadcasting Network (CBN) did almost daily reports about the dangers of the NHS. One report by CBN counted up the number of times George Washington was mentioned versus the Ku Klux Klan, while another looked at how often the NHS called George Washington the "Father of Our Country" versus his slaveowning legacy. Pat Robertson, founder of the 700 Club and head of CBN (also a multi-time Republican Presidential candidate), came out against the NHS, saying that the Standards were "unpatriotic" and neglected the great men and events important to American history. The Christian Coalition, the major sister organization of the 700 Club, also came out against the NHS at the end of 1994 and began to lobby Congress to denounce them.

If Pat Robertson and the Christian Coalition had been the only ones to come out against the NHS, Nash, Crabtree, and all involved in the project would have had a much easier time in gaining support for their recommendations. Robertson and the Christian Coalition, sad to say, were hardly alone in their assessment. The great pontificator Rush Limbaugh regularly attacked the NHS on his radio and now defunct television shows, while conservative columnist George Will wrote several editorials ripping the NHS to shreds. The National Council's biggest headache by far, however, was Lynne Cheney. Cheney was the former head of the NEH (1986–93) who had supported the development of the NHS in 1992 with a $525,000 grant.

In the fall of 1994, Cheney and her supporters went after the NHS as if it were the *Communist Manifesto*, writing editorials, doing radio interviews, issuing press releases, and giving speeches denouncing the NHS as multiculturalism gone awry. Cheney's editorial "The End of History," published in the *Wall Street Journal* on October 20, 1994, kicked off the debate with a preemptive strike on Nash and Crabtree. Cheney assaulted the NHS by asking her audience to imagine "an outline for the teaching of American history in which George Washington makes only a fleeting appearance and is never described as our first president. Or in which the foundings of the Sierra Club and the National Organization for Women are considered noteworthy events, but the first gathering of the U.S. Congress is not." Cheney's argument was essentially the same as Robertson's, but it gained political and educational legitimacy as a result of her voice. Cheney's qualifications as a policy maker (the former head of the NEH) and an educator made it difficult for many other educators and policy makers to take the NHS seriously. This was especially the case after she responded to charges of hypocrisy on the NHS issue by alleging that she had been "flim-flammed" by Nash, Crabtree, and the National Council for History Standards group.

Nash responded by going on the road to challenge Cheney's assertions in radio and conference debates. Although Nash's argument that the teaching of K-12 social studies/history would improve with a general focus on the histories of major racial, ethnic, and cultural groups instead of great WASP males was realistic and sound, he lost those debates. Nash lost in part because he fell victim to a classic problem that most scholars face in the public eye; he was unable to summarize his ideas into decent sound bytes. Nash and the National Council also lost partly because of the public's general distrust of university professors and their dispassionate examination of empirical facts and high-brow use of language. Cheney and her conservative supporters, with much more experience in the game that combines education, politics, and media manipulation, simply outgunned and outflanked Nash and Crabtree.

The fight over the NHS during 1994–95 was one of many factors that helped the Republicans take control of both Congressional houses in November 1994. One of the first acts of the Republican Right was to cut the NEH's budget to its lowest level in its thirty-year history. While this was merely the partial fulfillment of the Republican promise as part of their "Contract With America"—as Cheney, Bennett, and former House Speaker Newt Gingrich pushed to have the NEH eliminated—the NEH's support for the NHS and similar initiatives did not help. It did not matter that the National Council offered to and did revise the NHS in 1995. By the middle of 1995, as far as policy makers and educators were concerned, the NHS was a dead issue, as it was considered typical of the "Big Brother" government that Gingrich and his minions hoped to erase.

The worst that could happen to the NHS occurred not in an interview with Cheney outdebating Nash, but in a book by Nash, Crabtree, and another educator in Ross Dunn. Realizing they had failed to reach the American public with their argument about the need for a better and more inclusive history, Nash, Crabtree, and Dunn decided to discuss the NHS and their experiences as a result of their involvement in *History on Trial* (1997). Of course the book was meant for scholars, educators, and possibly the policy makers who had given them so much grief in 1994–95, not the general public (despite the authors' proclamations to the contrary). In *History on Trial*, Nash, Crabtree, and Dunn attempt to appease their critics and reach educators ambivalent about the NHS by divorcing it from multiculturalism. "Can a plurality of stories and jarring perspectives fit into a coherent understanding of the American past?," the authors ask. They explain that social history *"can* be mainstreamed readily enough by changing the governing narrative from the rise of democracy, defined in terms of electoral politics, to the struggle to fulfill the American ideals of liberty, equal justice, and equality" as "various groups [struggled] to elbow their way under the canopy of the nation's founding promises." They go further by also asking

> Can there be any grand narrative more powerful, coherent, democratic, and inspiring than the struggles of groups that have suffered discrimination, exploitation, and hostility but have overcome passivity and resignation to challenge their exploiters, fight for legal rights, resist and cross racial boundaries, and hence embrace and advance the American credo that 'all men are created equal?'…This is nothing less than the story of the uncompleted project of making Americanism 'a matter of heart and mind rather than race or ancestry.'"

By even asking these questions, Nash, et al. made the assumption that there needs to be a "single, coherent, integrated history" without realizing that the material they have described as social history is also in fact a multicultural one. Can anyone seriously say that a history that describes the "struggles of groups that have suffered discrimination, exploitation, and hostility" is not a multicultural one? Yet Nash, Crabtree, and Dunn not only suggested that these multiple struggles were not multicultural. They also asserted that the NHS would be a gigantic step toward assimilation. Nash, Crabtree, and Dunn, meanwhile, labeled multiculturalism merely as a "benign credo" and Afrocentricity as the dream of disillusioned left-wing militants who advocate "cultural separatism and aggrandizement that mirrored the self-glorifying Eurocentrism of earlier decades." Even in Nash's earlier discussions of multiculturalism, he was at least luke-warm to the idea of multiple perspectives on American history. Maybe the battering Nash, Crabtree, and Dunn had taken in the media wore on them, but by attacking Afrocentricity and dismissing multiculturalism, the authors essentially conceded victory to Cheney and those opposed to any changes in the Anglo-centered K-12 curriculum. It also meant that despite their efforts to salvage the NHS, Nash, Crabtree, and Dunn had killed virtually all of its remaining support.

Still, the NHS debate did not completely stall all efforts at reform, particularly in Afrocentric/Afrocentric-leaning circles. The controversies over African American male classrooms in Detroit, Baltimore, and Milwaukee and over Ebonics in Oakland, California between 1994 and 1997 are but two examples of attempts to change the Anglo-dominated curriculum through other means. Yet when a truly multicultural curriculum has been developed, it has not only been lumped with

Afrocentricity in order to delegitimize its potential advantages, but the curriculums have been fought with much more venom and ferocity. The controversies in the city and state of New York, and over the NHS nationally are all examples of 1990s-style bitter educational politics.

Minority Exclusion, Multiculturalism, and the One America Report:

The question that remains is whether all of these incidents add up to a formal educational policy. The answer is both no and yes. If one is seeking to find a statement from the U.S. Department of Education or the National Education Association on the merit and perils of multiculturalism (or even a definition), one then needs to stop searching. One simply is not going to find an explicit policy statement from a major national organization on multiculturalism in education. Nor can one look to federal agencies related to education for guidance here.

But if one reads between the lines of a certain White House initiative, then what policy makers think about multiculturalism in education might become a bit clearer. President Clinton's Initiative on Race, which started with widespread media coverage of the President's speech at the University of California, San Diego commencement on June 14, 1997, ended with a report buried in Monicagate obscurity on September 18, 1998. The initiative started with the promise of updating the Kerner Commission report (1968), which declared that "America was becoming two nations: one White, one Black, separate and unequal." President Clinton stated that the Initiative of Race was about making out "of our many different strands one America—a nation at peace with itself bound together by shared values and aspirations and opportunities and real respect for our differences." Declaring that "living in islands of isolation…is not the American way," President Clinton concluded his speech with the proposition that either we could become "many Americas, separate, unequal and isolated," or America could "draw strength from all [its] people…to become the world's first truly multi-racial democracy." Presumably, this "is the unfinished work of our time, to lift the burden of race and redeem the promise of America."

The seven-member Advisory Board included the trailblazing Black historian John Hope Franklin, former New Jersey governor Thomas Kean, former Mississippi governor William Winter, former CEO of Nissan Motor U.S.A. Robert Thomas, lawyer Angela Oh, Linda Chavez-Thompson (currently Democratic National Committee Vice Chair), and Bronx, New York minister Suzan Johnson Cook. Three White men, one African American man, one African American woman, one Hispanic woman, and one Asian American woman, all born between 1915 and 1957, made up the Advisory Board that would give America the blueprint for beginning a sincere dialogue on race. To say the least, the Advisory Board was not entirely representative of late-twentieth-century America. Despite each individual member's prior accomplishments, there are a host of other scholars, ministers, CEOs, lawyers, union organizers, and former governors who should have been considered for this task. Beyond that, the Advisory Board's lack of ideological (six liberals and one moderate) and age balance (the youngest person on the board was 41 in 1997) makes one wonder if they possessed broad enough perspectives to address race issues in 1968, much less during their 1997–98 tour on race.

The Advisory Board on Race—led by John Hope Franklin—traveled the nation in search of consensus but instead found controversy throughout their fifteen-month tenure. They produced a 229-page report titled *One America in the 21st Century*, which merely confirmed what most Americans would have already known: 1) that African Americans and other people of color continue to face economic and residential discrimination; 2) that public resources remain inequitably distributed along racial and ethnic lines (especially in public health and education); and 3) that police brutality continues to disproportionately impact African Americans and other persons of color. While the Advisory Board admitted that its report was "not a definitive analysis of the state of race relations in America today," almost any board could have catalogued the statistics of the thirty years since the Kerner Commission's report.

The Advisory Board asserted that in cris-crossing the country, they had "engage[d] the American people in a focused examination of how racial differences have affected our society and how to meet the racial challenges that face us." One of the Advisory Board's major goals was to promote a "constructive national dialogue to confront and work through the challenging issues that surround race." Chapter 1 and Appendix G of the *One America* speak to the issue of a constructive national dialogue on race, giving suggestions for any American interested in race relations regarding how to start a local town hall-style discussion of race.

All of this sounds wonderful on paper, and the Advisory Board seemed sincere in their suggestions. The only problem with what they recommended was that it was based on an implicit assumption: that all Americans know exactly what cultural values *all* Americans have in common. The Advisory Board apparently failed to see the inherent tension between discussing cultural similarities and differences—not to mention different group experiences in America, past and present—and then discussing how we must become one America in the 21st century. What is this notion of "one America" based on? The Advisory Board hinted that this notion is based on adhering to common beliefs in democracy, equality, and tolerance, all abstract ideas that are difficult for people to agree on even in the theoretically friendly context of a dialogue. All one can guess is that the Advisory Board fundamentally believed that Americans should put their cultural, racial, and ethnic differences aside to become *truly* American on the basis of important yet abstract concepts that all Americans may not fully believe in.

The Advisory Board, and Franklin specifically, could not even put aside its own differences across ideological lines to have their dialogues on race in America. Franklin refused to invite anti-affirmative action advocate Ward Connerly to an Advisory Board meeting regarding racial diversity on college campuses on November 20, 1997, which violated the spirit of the President's Initiative. Franklin stated that Connerly had "nothing to contribute" to the discussion on cultural differences. Connerly, a University of California regent, campaigned in 1996 for the passage of Proposition 209, which led directly to the repeal of all affirmative action programs for the state of California. This repeal has resulted in a decline in the number of Black and Hispanic students attending the University of California system.

Regardless of what one thinks of Connerly, President Clinton had charged Franklin and the rest of the Advisory Board to "join him in reaching out to local communities and listen to Americans from all different races and backgrounds." Clinton supposedly created this mandate "so that we can better understand the causes of racial tension"—not to increase them. The incident created an image of the Advisory Board as again being a group of ultra-liberal civil rights ideologues who have been unwilling to listen to disparate perspectives on race.

One also can infer how the Advisory Board treated the issue of cultural differences in their *One America* report. This issue was conspicuous by its virtual absence in the Advisory Board's comments about its report as well as in the *One America* report itself. The Advisory Board and its *One America* report did consistently harp on the need to recognize and celebrate cultural differences in a nation destined to be increasingly multiethnic in the 21st century. But this was not a discussion of cultural differences; this was merely a summary of what America has become demographically. Nowhere in the *One America* report will one find an examination of where key cultural differences lie, where cultural intersections exist, and which cultural differences could help move our country toward one united America. Simply stated, the Advisory Board never defined what they meant by "culture" or "cultural difference," and there was little analysis of whether cultural differences actually added to or subtracted from American society as a whole. The Advisory Board never even considered whether to treat culture as a static or fluid concept in their fifteen-month tour de force of friendly dialogues on race.

Significantly, the Advisory Board spent precious little time on the concept of multiculturalism from either a theoretical or practical perspective. The term is only found four times in the *One America* report; it is used to describe the work of grassroots organizations who promote racial and ethnic tolerance. The report does not contain a definition of multiculturalism, pluralism, or any related terms. The only thing that one can conclude from this is that the Advisory Board was never serious about addressing cultural differences in practical terms, or multiculturalism as a philosophical or theoretical basis for their report. The only thing that the Advisory Board was concerned about was providing a report chock full of social and economic statistics that provide evidence of continuing racial and ethnic inequalities and hope for the future, not in truly understanding the nature of cultural differences in American society. One really could not expect seven prominent persons with their own personal agendas and indifference regarding the Initiative on Race to create something useful on race relations for the twenty-first century. The Advisory Board itself was representative of America's past rather than what America ought to be both by ideology and by age. And how could the Advisory Board engage in a serious discussion on race when President Clinton's major motivation for the initiative was based on the need for a presidential legacy rather than the need to bridge the racial divide?

The embodiment of the Advisory Board's—and the Initiative's—lack of concern about understanding the increasing diversity of our society from a cultural perspective was President Clinton's commentary on his personal multicultural experiences:

> I am a Scotch-Irish Southern Baptist, and I'm proud of it. But my life has been immeasurably enriched by the power of the Torah, the beauty of the Koran, the piercing wisdom of the religions of East and South Asia—all embraced by my fellow Americans. I have felt indescribable joy and peace in Black and Pentecostal churches. I have come to love the intensity and selflessness of my Hispanic fellow Americans toward la familia. As a Southerner, I grew up on country music and county fairs and I still like them. But I have also reveled in the festivals and the food, the music and the art and the culture of Native Americans and Americans from every region in the world.

President Clinton, the Initiative on Race, the Advisory Board, and the subsequent *One America* report that represents his thinking, essentially boiled the complex issue of multiculturalism down into the McDonald's 1980s-era slogan of "food, folks, and fun." Clinton's statement was not only self-serving, it also served to turn cultural differences into racial and ethnic stereotypes. He defeated the purpose of having a dialogue on cultural differences in the first place.

Having an understanding of multiculturalism would have helped this Advisory Board in conducting their dialogues on race. This assumes, however, that the Advisory really did want to achieve a real dialogue on cultural differences and race. The only conclusion one can reach was that the Advisory Board was more concerned with finding an uncontroversial framework for discussion that would appease the President and the media and enable them to fulfill their mandate. The *One America* report is a sanitization of race and multiculturalism without really addressing what these terms have meant for America's past, what they mean today, and can mean in the twenty-first century. In the end, the report issued by the Advisory Board on Race did three things. It implicitly rejected multiculturalism as a viable philosophy for a dialogue on race and as a remedy to exclusion in education. It gave President Clinton the opportunity (which was squandered in Monicagate) to solidify a legacy as the "I Feel Your Pain" President in the midst of conservative dismissals of anything racial. And it reflected in subtle ways the previous three decades of conservative educational policy on the subjects of curriculum and culture.

Where do the last two decades of curriculum reform, debates about multiculturalism and Afrocentricity, and policy initiatives leave us? Extremely fatigued and confused, not to mention excluded from the educational reform process, angry at the mere mention of the term multiculturalism, and uncertain about the future of American education. A few things, though, are clear. Pundits, policy makers, politicians, and the media have willingly and unwittingly declared that multiculturalism is a pariah philosophy that will either destroy American education as we know it or just make a whole lot of people angry. We also know that African American scholars involved in advocating Afrocentricity have become "representative Negroes" for White America, meaning that all African Americans are true believers in the philosophy. And it is also clear that despite the general exclusion of everyday people of color and Americans as a whole, grassroots groups within urban school districts continue to fight for changes in a curriculum that even conservatives acknowledge (rightly or wrongly) is Anglo-centric.

Derrick Bell outlined what he calls the "Rules of Racial Standing" in his book *Faces At the Bottom of the Well* (1992). Among the five rules are that representatives of "the race" will only be heard if their ideas are in line with preconceived views of Black thought in White America, and that Whites will not listen to race men with other views. In the case of multiculturalism, this is absolutely true. Instead of James Banks repeatedly appearing on talk shows and on political panels to talk about and advise on multiculturalism, policy-making pundits such as Dinesh D'Souza and conservative sociologist Thomas Sowell have been given that role. Molefi Asante and Leonard Jeffries are exceptions only in the sense that their radically conservative notions of Afrocentricity as the promotion of racial superiority and positive self-esteem serve a larger purpose: to present African American thought as monolithic and not worthy of consideration. Even those who supposedly have racial standing because they are White—such as Christine Sleeter, Gary Nash, and Charlotte Crabtree—were inept at successfully connecting with the public about their ideas, confused multiculturalism with Afrocentricity themselves, or ignored the politics surrounding this issue until it was too late to get their message across.

All of this is linked to educational policy in the simplistic yet all too true reality that there is no educational policy in American society without educational politics. And with the direct connection between politics and the media, the public regardless of race rarely has the chance to participate in the larger debate about diversity and what that means for our schools and society in the twenty-first century. The Presidential Initiative on Race has for all intents and purposes declared that assimilation rules, and cultural differences important to understanding the twenty-first century American tapestry should be ignored.

This does not mean that multiculturalism is dead, that Afrocentricity will be the only curriculum reform involving culture and a few urban school districts, and that assimilation will win in the end. It is also obvious that there is little understanding of the fluidity of culture and the limitations of race as a social construct from the controversies mentioned here, as well as in our handling of 9/11. What the aforementioned does mean is that advocates for multiculturalism in education need to become more media savvy, better connected with the public and with the nuances of educational politics, and more aware that multiculturalism involves a war between fear and faith. The fear is that this increasingly diverse society will snatch the keys of culture and knowledge away from Anglophile gatekeepers and then marginalize them. The faith is that acknowledging the importance of cultural differences will help strengthen America's fragile civic institutions, fragile because they have failed to include all the various parts of America's culture and past.

Epilogue

A *New York Times* article from January 2000 reported that Wilber Wright College in Chicago had developed a "great books program" that was in its second year at the community college. The program is one that emphasizes the Western canon, as professors such as Bruce Gans have reasoned that with all the programs created for women, people of color, and gays/lesbians, it was time for a program geared to emphasize the achievements of White males. In establishing the "great books program"—amid the protests of some of Wright College's faculty and administrators—Professor Gans concluded that anything "you get out of something profound is better than getting 100 percent out of something of no significance."

While many of Gans' and Wright College's students are Black and Latino, this statement reflects a certain assumption that the great thinkers and writers of all time all have Western culture in common. Gans' argument also reveals another assumption, that students of color have barely tapped their potential to think deeply about the world around them because they have been given little exposure to classical Western texts. Gans is acting as a savior of Western culture by civilizing previously unexposed young Black and Brown minds to ideas supposedly unique to Europe and Europeans. It is this kind of response to the inclusion of African American and other non-White cultures that *Fear of a "Black" America* was written to address.

Let us begin again with what is *not* multiculturalism. It is not some backwater trickle-down theory from the Ivory Tower that constructs a utopian vision of American culture. Nor is multiculturalism the equivalent of Afrocentricity, although both have in common the basic premise that Western culture is far from the only great culture in the history or current composition of the world.

For African Americans during the twentieth century, multiculturalism was about the inclusion of the Black experience into what most agreed was an important but an exclusionary lily-White curriculum. Sure, many Blacks in Washington and elsewhere believed that African Americans should see themselves as "African" first (some would say first, second, and third) and "American" second. Others claimed that becoming fully "American" would be the *only* way Blacks could survive in America. But if one understands that multiculturalism as a practice for Blacks would mean that they acknowledge both their African and American essences, then to this extent many Blacks practiced multiculturalism during the twentieth century.

There were also significant class and gender issues embedded within the multicultural activities of African Americans. The thoughts of women like Anna Cooper—along with the ideas and actions of Felicia Chisley and Donna Potts—added a gendered dimension to multiculturalism in Black Washington. Class distinctions and interaction also enhanced and hindered multicultural activities within the African American community. But for all the elitism of Blacks such as Kelly Miller and Mary Church Terrell, many elites made positive contributions to the development of multiculturalism. It should also be noted that many of their ideas came through their interactions with ordinary Black Washingtonians.

Beyond Black Washington, African American intellectuals from Du Bois, Alain Locke, and Carter Woodson to James Banks and Asa Hilliard have all promoted the idea that a philosophy which respects both mainstream cultural values and the cultures of people of color would help level the playing field of American racial inequality. Although not everything these intellectuals put down on paper fits within the framework of multiculturalism, much of what they thought has made a difference in our understanding of multiculturalism today. These intellectuals, with all of their ideas and activities, help us bridge the activities of Black Washingtonians between 1925 and 1940 with the cultural activities of African American intellectuals during the Harlem Renaissance of the 1920s. These intellectuals also give us a wide view of how activities similar to what occurred in Black Washington also took place among Blacks in cities like New York, Philadelphia, and Chicago during the 1920s and 1930s. Whatever anyone believes about multiculturalism in its present form, one cannot deny that in the context of race—and to some extent in terms of gender and class—African American scholars helped shape multiculturalism from a philosophical and educational perspective.

Even with the development of multiculturalism among African Americans came the rise and fall of desegregation as the savior for Black equality and the ascendance of Afrocentricity as the cure-all for the exclusion of the Black experience. Western culture purists have taken advantage of Black activism in the areas of multiculturalism and Afrocentricity and made them one and the same for the American public. This deliberate linking of the two philosophies has resulted in the verbal street fights that have occurred between advocates and opponents of multiculturalism over the past two decades. This divisiveness has stagnated the movement toward cultural and educational inclusion within American education, particularly at the K-12 level. This is a sad reality, especially in light of the major demographic shifts that are in full bloom in American society. The rapid growth in population among Latinos and other groups of color relative to White Americans and a significant increase in interracial marriages have made it imperative to create an atmosphere of multicultural coexistence or oneness in American society.

How does one create an atmosphere of multiculturalism in American institutions and in society? The answer to this question begins unsurprisingly with American education. But American education cannot provide the answer in the way that educators and politicians have defined it during the twentieth century. Sure, we should change K-12 curricula to include the histories, cultures, and contributions of African Americans and other peoples of color in classes such as social studies/history, English, art, music—and to some extent in terms of contributions—math and the sciences. Yes, we have already introduced some of these changes to America's public schools in the past two decades. Revising a curriculum that has traditionally exalted the greatness of Western culture and the White American experience, however, is hardly enough to create an atmosphere of multiculturalism in America or level the playing field.

What should occur in using American education as one tool for multiculturalism goes well beyond K-12. Colleges and universities who train teachers must focus on preparing them for a multicultural world. This kind of work requires more than classes on how to develop lesson plans. Besides classes in pedagogy, we must raise requirements for the training of new teachers. This includes better grades, more majors in fields other than education at the undergraduate level, and more teachers with master's degrees. Raising standards for teachers also includes creating a weeding-out process so that only people who are well-trained and sincere in their commitment to students are the ones who become teachers. All of this can only occur if we pay teachers more money, but that is another book.

The hierarchy of public education must also change if one expects American education to shoulder a significant load in the multiculturalism process. Principals, guidance counselors, school superintendents, and other administrators should gain a better understanding of their communities and *who* is in their communities. They need to be more willing to work with teachers and allow them greater autonomy to discuss multicultural issues and foster multiculturalism. While administrators certainly have to respond to the wishes of their communities, they also should educate their communities about the need for a more inclusive curriculum and a more tolerant atmosphere.

If a multicultural curriculum is expected to work, then teachers must also change the way they see themselves, their profession, and their students. Teachers should become more proactive in changing the way the profession deals with issues of diversity. Sensitivity training classes alone will not create a teacher pool ready to work with all categories of Americans. Only teachers who desire to work with students of varied social, economic, and ethnic backgrounds should be allowed to teach these populations. Combined with longer and better training, higher pay, and the creation of new funding streams for schools apart from local property taxes, K-12 public education and its teachers could play a vital role in making multiculturalism come alive.

Yet schools alone cannot change the way people think and feel about each other. Schools for the past century have operated both as a vehicle for societal change and as a mirror of societal values and attitudes. In the case of D.C. Public Schools, both views of education are completely accurate. What might be different in D.C. Public Schools' case was that the school district before 1954 played an almost exclusive role as the guardian of the status quo (i.e., segregation and inequitable distribution of resources). Black (and White) Washingtonians pressured the school system's change and reform during the late-1940s and 1950s. Even after the end of legal segregation in the District schools, new problems developed which have curtailed reforms called for by the school district. Despite the tremendous power of the District community in pushing for reforms, the school district continues to face serious financial problems, acute teacher shortages, and low student achievement.

If multiculturalism is a philosophy that can promote both diversity and unity in twenty-first century America, then other institutions and arenas within American society must shoulder the responsibility for incorporating this philosophy. From the American workplace to American cultural institutions to American government, multiculturalism could impact the subtle forms of exclusion and discrimination which continue to plague them. These institutions must possess the attitude that an atmosphere of cultural (more than demographic) diversity and inclusion for all of their best and brightest is of the utmost importance. Demographic diversity (i.e., hiring and working with the best people regardless of race/ethnicity) without addressing the climate or culture of a previously homogeneous institution leads neither to diversity nor to a productive workplace. From museums to the media, there needs to be a shift from demographic inclusion to the full infusion of diverse cultural attitudes and activities within their institutional cultures.

Then there are America's religious institutions and multiculturalism. Certainly xenophobia would remain alive and well in America's churches, synagogues, mosques, and temples long after multiculturalism is added to America's public schools. Our post-9/11 times reflect this unfortunate reality with regard to American Muslims and Sikhs. As one matriarch of White supremacy described it in the July 2000 *20/20* story "Right Women," the Ku Klux Klan and Christianity are linked in a seamless tapestry of Caucasian pride and hatred. Despite this reality, the growth of interracial and nondenominational churches and congregations gives one hope that American believers in a higher power will one day practice what is usually preached.

American religious institutions, in the meantime, must also conduct their own self-examinations to find out if their teachings on the fallibility of human beings also contain tinges of racism, sexism, and elitism. This is especially necessary for those of the Christian faith (Catholic, Protestant, Nondenominational) precisely because they remain part of America's dominant belief system. Although Americans have the right to worship (or not worship) as they wish, it need not come at the expense of someone else's rights. One cannot speak of the universal sameness of humankind under God and in the same breath claim God's Whiteness or Blackness—or declare that some groups cannot become one with God—without sounding like hypocrites.

Despite his many inconsistencies, Jesse Jackson's work in establishing Operation PUSH in Chicago during the 1970s and the Rainbow Coalition during the 1980s was partly an extension of the idea that regardless of difference, people with common spiritual and material concerns should collaborate to solve each other's problems. Jackson's Rainbow Coalition also embodied the notion that *because* of difference, groups with various concerns could contribute unique perspectives that would unravel persistent problems. Jackson's occasional grandstanding and overblown "Hymietown" comments aside, he has endeavored over the past thirty years to bring Black and White, Christian and Jew, rich and poor together to address America's greatest dilemmas. One must acknowledge that there was a religious or spiritual component that motivated Jackson's actions (he is, after all, an ordained minister) in establishing Operation PUSH and the Rainbow Coalition in the first place.

Of course, this is only one national example out of the many localized ones of people from varying backgrounds working on a spiritual basis to resolve material crises. Between the Religious Right's push to dismantle the Civil Rights era's legacy and avowed "Christian" White supremacists who burn Black churches and kill gay men, however, one wonders if America's Christians possess the capacity to turn God's love into secular action. Regardless of what one thinks of religion and Christianity in particular, there is little chance of multiculturalism becoming a true philosophical reality in American life without the church (Black, Brown, White, Catholic, Protestant, and Nondenominational) emphasizing a tough-minded, multiculturalism-based love. This kind of love requires a faith that realizes—despite significant obstacles and differences—that all must participate in correcting the racial, economic, educational, and cultural wrongs in American society if American society is expected to survive and thrive.

The American media could play one of the key roles in transmitting multiculturalism as a philosophical ideal in American society, in addition to its own creeds of freedom, democracy, and fairness. Up to this point, however, the media has been anything but friendly toward multiculturalism. Cases such as the National History Standards and new curriculum proposals in New York State and City illustrate that the media is not objective in its coverage of multiculturalism. Sure, the media and journalists have been objective in the sense that they have neither endorsed nor written off multiculturalism in education or in any other arena in American society. The way the press and the media have framed multiculturalism as this "thing" that came out of nowhere and began the "culture wars" of the late-1980s and 1990s, on the other hand, is anything but objective. Almost every article published in or written by the press on multiculturalism frames it in an antagonistic manner, without any thought of seeking a definition for multiculturalism or learning about its history. Radio and television coverage has been even worse, for it depicts the major players on both sides of the issue as opposing teams playing in the Super Bowl without engaging the public in a serious discussion of what ultimately is at stake.

Almost as bad as the media's coverage of multiculturalism is the media's coverage of people of color. Not that there is not any representation of Blacks, Latinos, or other people of color in newspapers and magazines, or on television and radio, but much of what is presented to the public is superficial and negative. People of color are portrayed in the media as brutal criminals, long-suffering victims, or superachievers who somehow transcended race to become successful in America. These depictions are mere caricatures of who these people of color truly are, the circumstances that they have faced, and the activities (good and bad) that they have engaged in to make the news in the first place. It appears that the media is just as disconnected from the understanding of race and culture as the professors discussed in the previous chapter.

For starters, African Americans, Latinos, and other people of color should insist on a media and a press that is more responsive to their needs and presents their communities in a more complete light. This does not necessarily mean a more positive light, but it does require obtaining a more panoramic view of who African Americans and other people of color are and what issues are important to them. The media and journalistic attitude that "if it bleeds it leads" and that a story must be adversarial in order to gain public interest must be replaced with a more constructive relationship with the public. Those in the media and in the press who contend that a reporter must be objective, dispassionate, and independent from the public have obviously forgotten that they are fallible human beings who are also part of the American body politic. Attempting to do good journalism or to raise news ratings is fine as long as one engages the public—the whole public. Until the media and the press acknowledge that they need to be more proactive in their work with the public (especially people of color), their coverage will remain a facade of objectivity and a disservice to the American public. Their ratings and readership will also continue to decline.

Part of this proactive and facilitatory process of framing and reporting the news would require a more multicultural atmosphere within the media and the press. In other words, stories about the importance of the Black middle class in late-twentieth century America, for example, would not just run during Black History Month. Articles about the significance of the Latino vote and culture would not just be reported when a politician who happens to be the brother of someone married to a person of Latino descent rolls into town. Reports about the widening achievement gap between high-achieving Asian students and everyone else would not just come out with the issuing of the latest SAT statistics. There are more issues and ideas beyond these kinds of reports about people of color. Being multicultural in this case simply requires editors, journalists, and media reporters to dig deeper, to appreciate complexity, and to understand that there is much they do not understand about the diversity of the people they cover in their stories. For the twenty-first century media and press, it is of paramount importance that they seek to connect the disconnected, and to become more culturally and intellectually diverse as they become more demographically diverse.

Although government as an institution has been a vanguard for demographic diversity over the past three and a half decades, it has done little on the issue of cultural diversity, with the assumption that all cultures would assimilate into the mainstream. If one truly believes that this has actually happened at this point in the story, then one is completely out of touch with reality. Government at all levels should lead in changing an atmosphere of blandness into one that truly appreciates America's multicultural fabric.

Law enforcement and criminal justice are in need of serious cultural reform, probably more so than any other set of government institutions. Stories of more racial profiling (including "Driving While Black"), an increase in police brutality, the release of death row inmates (mostly Black and Hispanic) from prison after the courts overturned their wrongful convictions, and corruption scandals involving dozens of police officers have all abounded in the last ten years. Cities such as New York, Los Angeles, Pittsburgh, Philadelphia, and Baltimore, counties such as Montgomery and Prince George's Counties in Maryland, and states like New Jersey and Illinois have all been involved in all of these unnerving incidents. From Rodney King's videotaped beating at the hands of LAPD's finest in 1991 to Anthony Porter's overturned conviction after coming within two days of his execution in Illinois in 1999, the law enforcement and criminal justice systems continue to discriminate against and brutalize people of color. Over 200 prisoners had their convictions thrown out as a result of the LAPD corruption scandal, and at least a dozen death row inmates have been released from prison in Illinois after the discovery of new evidence proving their innocence. Almost all of these men are Black and Brown.

In New York City, there are two recent cases that highlight how disconnected people of color are from even-handed law enforcement and true justice. The Abner Louima case (1999) that began in August 1997 when four New York police officers brutalized the Haitian immigrant in their station house with a broomstick was topped in February 1999 by the killing of Amadou Diallo at his doorstep. Diallo's crime was being a Black man who was wanted for questioning in a rape case involving a White woman. Forty-one bullets and a acquittal later, the only reasonable explanation for the shooting is that four White police officers saw a "suspicious" looking Black man, and they decided to shoot first and ask questions later. While three of the four officers involved in the Louima case were convicted and sentenced to serve time in prison, it took the testimony of another White officer engrossed in the crime who cut a deal to put the other three there. One of these convictions was later overturned.

The answer to these deep-rooted problems is much more complicated than police departments hiring more people of color. Over the past four decades, urban police departments have become more demographically diverse, although not in proportion to the urban populations they are sworn to protect and serve. Even if more diversity eventually brought police departments to par demographically with their communities, it would not end police brutality or racial profiling. The way one destroys the blue wall of silence and corruption is by changing the *culture* of law enforcement from the ground up, with multicultural ideas *and* people.

The same is true of the American criminal justice system. With prisoners of color making up more than eighty percent of all death row inmates, it seems that the criminal justice system should take more precautions to protect the rights of America's accused and convicted, especially in light of the LAPD corruption scandal. The non-White, poor, and uneducated are at a distinct disadvantage in a system that first concentrates their search for criminals on those in their ranks, and then incarcerates these individuals without the benefit of a thorough investigation of their cases. Multiculturalism in this context simply means that African Americans, Hispanics, and other people of color are entitled to the same constitutional and civil rights that their middle class White counterparts are assumed to possess when they come in contact with law enforcement and the criminal justice system. Multiculturalism here would also be the hiring and promotion of more district attorneys of color, more judges of color, a jury system that does not assume jury nullification on the basis of race, and the treatment of our American body of law as a fluid and changeable system of precepts. This would at least begin to level the playing field of criminal justice so that all Americans regardless of race or ethnicity can truly retain the right of innocence until their guilt is proven, as well as a fair trial with a competent attorney.

But this alternative reality seems further away than ever with the post-9/11 detention of Arab Americans and others of Middle Eastern descent without due process at Guantanamo Bay. Not to mention the brutalizing of Iraqi prisoners at Abu Ghraib. What this says is that expecting justice for people of color from a fearful White majority is a fleeting proposition at home and abroad.

Those who still think multiculturalism is a horrible philosophy spawned by Satan might believe that multiculturalism could be used to bring an end to another evil—affirmative action. But this depends on how one sees affirmative action. If one believes it has kept qualified Whites from going to the college of their choice or obtaining their ideal job, then multiculturalism implies that everyone will be treated the same. The assumption here, of course, is that Whites are the most qualified people for positions of status in higher education, in the workplace, and in society. If one assumes that affirmative action is absolutely necessary to ensure that Blacks, women, and other persons of color have the opportunity to attend college or to obtain a job, then multiculturalism might be seen as a philosophy that could enhance the chances of non-Whites for things assumed to be the birthright of affluent Whites. The counterargument here is that women benefit more than people of color from affirmative action, and that middle class Blacks benefit more from it than working-class/poor African Americans. While affirmative action in its current or future form is necessary to minimize discrimination in education and employment, multiculturalism works on the attitudes that create the need for affirmative action in the first place. Whereas affirmative action's implications are limited to middle class professionals, the long-term impact of multiculturalism would reach every institution in America.

Surely one does not teach multiculturalism, one practices it. Although one can teach students about multiculturalism as a philosophy and incorporate it in a curriculum, it is the practice of multiculturalism that is the most important for American society. Every encounter with someone different from oneself and one's culture that leads to serious dialogue informs one about themselves, the other person, and that other person's culture. Putting this specifically in the context of mid-twentieth century Black Washington, multicultural practice occurred daily within this community, even between Black and White Washingtonians. This was partly because Blacks had to operationalize it, and partly because of an increased Black consciousness towards understanding difference and heritage during the 1920s and 1930s. Modeling multiculturalism is what will make a multicultural curriculum work, not the elimination of Western cultural purists.

In the case of those who firmly believe that Afrocentricity is the ultimate answer to the cultural dilemma facing African Americans today, there is still a place for this perspective in a truly multicultural America. Unlike the arguments of Western culture gatekeepers such as Arthur Schlesinger, Diane Ravitch, William Bennett, Dinesh D'Souza, the assertion here is that one should not throw the baby out with the bathwater. Just because some of the advocates and ideas related to Afrocentricity can be seen as distasteful does not mean that the whole philosophy is polluted. For all the greatness of Western culture, it has also produced modern slavery, mass warfare and pollution, and the scientific racism that led to the rise of Hitler, World War II, and nuclear weapons. And despite the greatness of Western culture, there appears to be some evidence that ancient Greek civilization was influenced in part by ancient Egyptian and Phoenician civilizations. To put it another way, Western culture has not exactly been "all that" for Blacks and other people of color, not to mention women and the poor. This is true even if one concedes that principles fundamental to Western culture like equality and democracy have made it possible for groups of color and women to raise their status in the last four decades. Few scholars or pundits (including Afrocentrists), however, would suggest that all of Western culture's philosophical underpinnings be tossed aside because of a few crackpots and their warped ideas.

If one takes the arguments of Schlesinger, Ravitch, Bennett, D'Souza, and Lynne Cheney seriously, then the one thing that we must conclude is that America has much work to do on the cultural front. Because if one truly examines their arguments—that multiculturalism equals Afrocentricity, is divisive, and Western cultural purity must be preserved at all costs—one would see that there is not much difference between them and the views of White supremacy groups. Yes, this statement might seem a bit extreme, but only if one is actually accusing these very accomplished scholars, educators, and policy makers of deliberate bigotry or racism. There is not much difference, on the other hand, between an argument for the preservation of the Western canon and the total assimilation of "other" cultures and one that advocates the purity of the White race. Both arguments are based in fear and the belief that because Western culture has expanded its influence over the past half-millennium, it is automatically better.

At the same time, one could argue that Afrocentrists who offer the sometimes radically reactionary theories they have constructed are deliberately attempting to make White Americans even more uncomfortable than they already are about Blacks and Black culture. Statements about the worthlessness of Western culture to African Americans, studies that idealize ancient Egypt, and theories describing the mystical powers of melanin are laughable to many African Americans, but scare many Whites. The answer here is not to write books and make speeches denouncing Afrocentricity and other so-called ethnocentricities. By attacking rabid proponents of Afrocentricity, Western cultural purists are giving even their most hair-brained ideas validity. There is also the implicit assumption that all African Americans somehow must all be supporters of Afrocentricity. It is an assumption that drives many to defend the philosophy, many who otherwise would not give it the time of day. Time should instead be the judge of the overall validity of Afrocentricity for Blacks, for that is what ultimately determines the soundness of any philosophy.

In the end, will multiculturalism work? That depends on what one expects of multiculturalism. If the expectation is that multiculturalism will help boost the self-esteem of people of color, then it will not be of any use to American education or society. While no one in society should have the right to devalue the significance of others' cultures in any tangible way, it is not the job of our society to make people feel good about their culture. If a major side effect of multiculturalism is the raising of self-esteem, then it is a wonderful philosophy that binds us together as it defines our differences. Raising self-esteem is not the primary focus of multiculturalism.

Defining differences and commonalities, creating a dialogue for discussion of deeply rooted and difficult societal issues, and establishing a more complete historical record are all part of multiculturalism's agenda. In the American context, the ultimate goal of multiculturalism's advocates is to take the phrase *e pluribus unum* ("out of the many one") and encourage America to live up to this creed. Anglophile purists such as Schlesinger, Bennett, and Ravitch believe that this creed really means "America is one no matter what differences exist" between Americans. This oneness, of course, comes at the price of checking one's diversity at the door of opportunities dominated by WASP values that many consider static and unchangeable.

But if one understands that America is more than a nation that molds immigrants into a homogeneous piece of steel, then one knows that America more than anything else is an experiment. If the Founding Fathers deserve credit for any *one* thing, it would be for creating founding documents that were designed for revision and change over time. Both the Declaration of Independence and the Constitution were intended as living documents guaranteeing every citizen certain "unalienable rights such as life, liberty, and the pursuit of happiness." Keeping this in mind, it is really difficult to justify an argument for cultural assimilation in America, as assimilation might violate the basic premise for the establishment of American society, a "more perfect union" between all Americans.

In this post-industrial, early twenty-first century American context, the notions of one America and multiculturalism are not at all separate ones. If one wants the racial divide to close along cultural, educational, and other lines, then one needs to acknowledge cultural differences based on the Americans experiences of people of color. Saying that Americans should all become one culturally ignores the good, the bad, and the sometimes ugly history regarding race and difference in American society. It also ignores the cultural baggage that all groups have brought to American society throughout our history.

There is one final question that needs to be asked here: can multiculturalism help America completely transcend our racial and ethnic divide? No, it cannot. It cannot because the transcendence of race for many Americans would mean looking beyond or ignoring our differences rather than acknowledging and embracing difference. Transcendence might also mean oversimplifying or stereotyping differences so that someone like Michael Jordan or Bob Costas becomes raceless or cultureless to most Americans. This vision of transcendence would homogenize American culture while sweeping diversity underneath a rug; in some circles, it already has. As Michael Eric Dyson suggests in *Race Rules*, transcendence of race or culture still implies that being a person of color or of a different culture is unacceptable. The only way America will "transcend" race is through embracing diversity, and American can only do that through recognizing the fluidity and complexity of culture and understanding the importance of pluralism even in our more xenophobic times.

To answer the question this book began with—"What is multicultural-ism?"—one must acknowledge that it is a philosophy that is consistent with American ideals and imperative to the improvement of American education. Multiculturalism is America's best hope for inclusion without homogenization and for building a bridge across the chasm of racial and ethnic divisions. Without multiculturalism, the problem of the twenty-first century will bring Du Bois's issue at the beginning of the twentieth to a head. The "problem of the color line," as Du Bois put it, will become the problem of the culture line in the twenty-first century, one that could possibly be even more violent than the twentieth century if American continues to insist on a WASP construction of cultural importance. The verdict on the Diallo shooting in New York State and the Homeland Secu-rity Act are just two signs of color and cultural differences and White America's fear of diversity. The way America has been cannot be the way many want it to be for the twenty-first century, not with multiculturalism offering the promise of an enriching thread for the thread-bare American tapestry.

Notes

FEAR OF A "BLACK" AMERICA AND MULTICULTURALISM

[12] *"...could spend...entire life without..."* "Rage," *Law & Order [Television Series]*, Episode 101, 1 February 1995.

[18] *"Melting pot theory," "Assimilation," and "Bilingual education"* See Philip Gleason, *Speaking of Diversity: Language and Ethnicity in Twentieth-Century America* (Baltimore: Johns Hopkins University, 1992), Chapter 1; Christina Bratt Paulston, *Bilingual Education: Theories and Issues* (Rowley, MA: Newbury House Publishers, 1980); and United States Commission on Civil Rights, *A Better Chance to Learn: Bilingual Bicultural Education, Clearinghouse Publication No. 51* (Washington: Government Printing Office, May 1975).

[19] *Newsweek* dedicated an entire issue in September 1991 to the controversy over Afrocentricity in American education and the origins of classical civilization. For more, see: "African Dreams [Cover Story]," *Newsweek*, 23 September 1991; and Martin Bernal, *Black Athena: The Afroasiatic Roots of Classical Civilization, Volumes 1 and 2* (New Brunswick, NJ: Rutgers University Press, 1987/1991).

Sam Howe Verhovek, "Plan to Emphasize Minority Cultures Ignites A Debate," *New York Times*, 21 June 1991, A1, A3; Gary Putka, "Curricula of Color," *The Wall Street Journal*, 1 July 1991, A1, A4; Joseph Berger, "Arguing About America," *New York Times*, 21 June 1991; New York State Education Department, *One Nation, Many Peoples: A Declaration of Cultural Interdependence* (Albany, NY: The Report of the New York State Social Studies Review and Development Committee, 1991); Schlesinger, *Disuniting of America*; William J. Bennett, *Our Children and Our Country: Improving America's Schools and Affirming the Common Culture* (New York: Simon and Schuster, 1988); Diane Ravitch, "Diversity and Democracy: Multicultural Education in America," *American Scholar* 59 (Spring 1990): 10-14; and "Multiculturalism: E Pluribus Plures," *American*

Scholar 59 (Summer, 1990): 337-54; and Thomas Sowell, *Inside American Education: The Decline, The Deception, The Dogmas* (New York: Free Press, 1993).

[20] *"Audiences come to popular culture with a past..."* Levine, "The Folklore of Industrial Society: Popular Culture and Its Audiences," *American Historical Review* 97 (December 1992), 1381–82.

"Authentically..." Robin D. G. Kelley, "Notes on Deconstructing 'The Folk,'" *American Historical Review* 97 (December 1992): 1400–08.

[21] See Tricia Rose, *Black Noise: Rap Music and Black Culture in Contemporary America* (Middletown, CT: Wesleyan University Press, 1994); Rose and Andrew Ross, eds., *Microphone Fiends: Youth Music & Youth Culture* (New York: Routledge, 1994); Nelson George, *Buppies, B-boys, Baps & Bohos: Notes on Post-Soul Black Culture, 1st Edition* (New York: HarperCollinsPublishers, 1992); Bakari Kitwana, *The Hip-Hop Generation: Young Blacks and The Crisis in African-American Culture* (New York: BasicCivitas Books, 2002); and Leon E. Wynter, *American Skin: Pop Culture, Big Business & The End of White America* (New York: Crown Publishers, 2002).

Joe William Trotter, Jr., *Coal, Class, and Color: Blacks in Southern West Virginia, 1915–32* (Urbana: University of Illinois Press, 1990), 51-52, 254-57; Earl Lewis, *In Their Own Interests: Race, Class, and Power in Twentieth-Century Norfolk, Virginia* (Berkeley: University of California Press, 1991), 39; and Robin D. G. Kelley, "'We Are Not What We Seem': Rethinking Black Working-Class Opposition in the Jim Crow South," *Journal of American History* 80 (June 1993): 77-78. See also James C. Scott, *Domination and the Arts of Resistance: Hidden Transcripts* (New Haven: Yale University Press, 1990)., 183.

[22] *"Desegregation" and "Integration"* Harold Cruse, *Plural But Equal: A Critical Study of Blacks and Minorities and America's Plural Society* (New York: William Morrow, 1987), 22-24; and Banks, "The Canon Debate, Knowledge Construction, and Multicultural Education," *Educational Researcher* 22 (June/July 1993): 4-14.

[23] *"While not all leaders were intellectuals..."* August Meier, *Negro Thought in America, 1880–1915: Racial Ideologies in the Age of Booker T. Washington* (Ann Arbor: University of Michigan Press, 1963); Meier and Elliott Rudwick, *Black History and the Historical Profession, 1915–1980* (Urbana: University of Illinois

Press, 1986); and Meier and John Hope Franklin, eds., *Black Leaders of the Twentieth Century* (Urbana: University of Illinois Press, 1982).

"...instill race pride..." Donald E. Collins, Interview with Felicia Chisley, 13 October 1995, Washington, D.C.

24 *"cultural pluralism..."* Gleason, *Speaking of Diversity*, Chapter 2.

"...a peculiar sensation..." W. E. B. Du Bois, *The Souls of Black Folk* (New York: Penguin Books, 1993; 1903), 45; David Levering Lewis, *W. E. B. Du Bois: Biography of a Race, 1868–1919* (New York: H. Holt and Company, 1993), 281.

25 *"...university education of black men in the United States..."* Du Bois, *The Education of Black People: Ten Critiques, 1906–1960* (New York: Monthly Review Press, 1973), 95; Carter G. Woodson, *The Mis-education of the Negro* (Washington: Associated Publishers, 1933), 145-50.

26 *"Negro life is seizing upon its first chances..."* Nathan I. Huggins, *Harlem Renaissance* (New York: Oxford University Press, 1971), 57-59; Alain Locke, ed., *The New Negro: An Interpretation* (New York: Albert and Charles Boni, 1925), 3-16; Locke, *Race Contacts and Interracial Relations*, 96-97.

Rutledge M. Dennis, "Relativism and Pluralism in the Social Thought of Alain Locke," in Russell J. Linnemann, ed., *Alain Locke: Reflections on a Modern Renaissance Man* (Baton Rouge: Louisiana State University Press, 1982), 31-32; and Horace M. Kallen, "Alain Locke and Cultural Pluralism," *Journal of Philosophy* 54 (February 1957), 120.

HEADY DAYS

30 See the following: Nathan I. Huggins, *Harlem Renaissance* (New York: Oxford University Press, 1971); Judith Stein, *The World of Marcus Garvey: Race and Class in Modern Society* (Baton Rouge: Louisiana State University Press, 1986); and David L. Lewis, *When Harlem Was In Vogue* [2nd Edition] (New York: Oxford University Press, 1989).

"...held steadfastly to the hope..." Gatewood, *Aristocrats of Color*, 39, 45, 67-68; and Lewis, *When Harlem Was In Vogue*, xvi.

[32] Alain L. Locke, ed., *The New Negro: Voices of the Harlem Renaissance* (New York: Albert and Charles Boni, 1925), xxv, 3-4.

[33] *"...foresee changes in the world"* W. E. B. Du Bois, *The Education of Black People: Ten Critiques, 1906–1960* (New York: Monthly Review Press, 1973), 65-66, 68-73; and *The Autobiography of W. E. B. Du Bois: A Soliloquy on Viewing My Life from the Last Decade of Its First Century* (New York: International Publishers, 1968), 296-97, 305; and Frederick D. Dunn, "African-American Philosophy and Philosophies of Education: Their Roots, Aims and Relevance for the 21st Century" (Ed.D. Dissertation, Columbia University, 1991), 106-108, 112.

[34] *"...neither of the older selves to be lost..."* David Levering Lewis, *W. E. B. Du Bois: Biography of a Race* (New York: H. Holt, 1993), 238-67, 281-83, and *W. E. B. Du Bois: The Fight for Equality and the American Century, 1919–1963* (New York: Henry Holt & Company, 2000); Du Bois, *Souls of Black Folk*, 76-77, 138; Du Bois, *Writings*, 133, 144, 365.

[36] *"...outthinking and outflanking the owners of the world today..."* Du Bois, *Education of Black People*, 76-77.

[37] Lewis, *When Harlem Was In Vogue*, xvi, 49; Du Bois, *Black Reconstruction: An Essay Toward a History of the Part Which Black Folk Played in the Attempt to Reconstruct Democracy in America* (Chicago: University of Chicago Press, 1935), 713.

[38] *"...if we are going to use history for our pleasure..."* Du Bois, *Black Reconstruction*, 714, 722, 724.

[41] Jacqueline Goggin, *Carter G. Woodson: A Life in Black History* (Baton Rouge: Louisiana State University Press, 1993), 7-26.

[42] *"Negro institutions of learning and those of Whites, too..."* Carter G. Woodson, "The Miseducation of the Negro," *Crisis* 38 (August 1931), 266-67; Goggin, "Carter G. Woodson and the Collection of Source Materials for Afro-American History," *American Archivist* 158 (Summer 1985): 261-71; and Patricia W. Romero, "Carter G. Woodson: A Biography" (Ph.D. Dissertation, Ohio State University, 1971), 132-38.

[43] *"Taught from the books of the same bias..."* Woodson, *The Mis-education of the Negro* (Washington: Associated Publishers, 1933), xii-xiii, 15, 17, 22-23, 145.

[44] *"...in advanced work on Shakespeare..."* Woodson, *Mis-education of the Negro*, 118-19, 144, 146-47, 150, 154, 192.

"Thousands Drawn to Negro History Week Programs," *Washington Tribune*, 2 November 1933, 16.

[45] *"...the best there is in our racial character..."* Joseph J. Rhoads, "Teaching the Negro Child," *Journal of Negro History* 19 (January 1934), 15, 16-17, 19-21; Arthur D. Wright, "What We should Teach the Negro Child about Himself and about Others in Relation to Himself," 32-33, 35-37.

[46] *"...displacement of the Negro in skilled and unskilled labor..."* Herman Dreer, "The Education of the Negro with Respect to His Background," *Journal of Negro History* 19 (January 1934), 45; and Benjamin Brawley, "The Promise of Negro Literature," 53, 56.

Woodson, "We Have Never Made an Actual Fight Against Segregation, Says Woodson," 10 February 1934, 4; "Teaching the Negro Deliberately and Specifically About His Achievements," 11 January 1934, 4; "Varying Conceptions of History," 15 February 1934, 4; "Truth in the Battle with Error," 5 April 1934, 4; and "What Aspect of Negro Life and History would You Dramatize?," 27 December 1935, 8.

[47] *"...a traitor to his race..."* "Calls DuBois a Traitor If He Accepts Post," *Washington Afro-American*, 30 May 1936, 2; "No $8,000-Job Offer—Woodson," 30 May 1936, 3; and Carter G. Woodson, "New Encyclopedia Project Gets Slap from Woodson," 27 June 1936, 19. See also: "Dr. Brawley Disagrees With Dr. Woodson," *Washington Afro-American*, 30 May 1936, 6.

Frederick D. Dunn, "The Educational Philosophies of Washington, Du Bois, and Houston: Laying the Foundations for Afrocentrism and Multiculturalism," *Journal of Negro Education* 62 (Winter 1993): 24-34; August Meier and Elliott Rudwick, "Carter G. Woodson as Entrepreneur: Laying the Foundation of a Historical Specialty," in Meier and Rudwick, *Black History and the Historical Profession, 1915–1980* (Urbana: University of Illinois Press, 1986), 1-73; James Turner and C. Steven McGann, "Black Studies as an Integral Tradition in African-American Intellectual History," *Journal of Negro Education* 49 (Winter 1980): 52-59; and Samuel Hay, "Carter G. Woodson's *Mis-education of the Negro*: A Re-Visit," *Negro History Bulletin* 38 (1975): 436-49.

[48] *"...sought to demythologize and demystify..."* Werner Sollors, Caldwell Titcomb, and Thomas A. Underwood, eds., *Blacks at Harvard: A Documentary History of African-American Experience at Harvard and Radcliffe* (New York: New York University Press, 1993), 129-30; and Leonard Harris, ed., *The Philosophy of Alain Locke: Harlem Renaissance and Beyond* (Philadelphia: Temple University Press, 1989), 3-4.

Rutledge M. Dennis, "Relativism and Pluralism in the Social Thought of Alain Locke," in Russell J. Linnemann, ed., *Alain Locke: Reflections on a Modern Renaissance Man* (Baton Rouge: Louisiana State University Press, 1982), 31-32; and Horace M. Kallen, "Alain Locke and Cultural Pluralism," *Journal of Philosophy* 54 (February 1957), 120.

[49] *"The goal of race progress and race adjustment..."* Alain LeRoy Locke, *Race Contacts and Interracial Relations: Lectures On The Theory And Practice Of Race*, Jeffrey Stewart, ed., (Washington: Howard University Press, 1992), xix-xl, 94-95, 99; Lewis, *When Harlem Was in Vogue*, 149-50.

[50] *"All classes of people under social pressure..."* Locke, "The New Negro," in Alain LeRoy Locke, ed., *The New Negro*, 3, 5-6; and Locke, "Youth Speaks," *Survey Graphic* 6 (March 1925), 659.

[51] Mia Bay, *The White Image in the Black Mind: African-American Ideas about White People, 1830–1925* (New York: Oxford University Press, 2000), 198-99.

[54] *"...center for the research study..."* Rayford W. Logan, *Howard University: The First Hundred Years, 1867–1967* (New York: New York University Press, 1969), 250-51, 274-77; and Locke to Mordecai Johnson, Memorandum on Department of African Studies at Howard University, 5 June 1928, 1-4, in *Alain LeRoy Locke Papers*, Box 164-105, Moorland-Spingarn Research Collection, Howard University.

[52] *"...in sample social experiences with the life and folkways of minority groups."* Alain Locke, "Minorities and the Social Mind," *Progressive Education* 12 (March 1935): 141-45.

[53] Locke, "The Character and Significance of Negro History in a Liberal Arts College," 1930s, 1-3, in *Alain Locke Papers*, Boxes 164-141 and 164-142, Moorland-Spingarn Research Center, Howard University; and Locke and Bernhard J.

Stern, eds., *When Peoples Meet: A Study in Race and Culture Contacts* (New York: Progressive Education Association, 1942).

[53] *"...incorporates racial, cultural, sexual...considerations."* Elsa Barkley Brown, "Womanist Consciousness: Maggie Lena Walker and the Independent Order of Saint Luke," *Signs* 14 (Fall 1989), 611-12; Gloria Ladson-Billings, "Lifting As We Climb: The Womanist Tradition in Multicultural Education," in James A. Banks, ed., *Multicultural Education, Transformative Knowledge, and Action* (New York: Teachers College Press, 1996), 182-83; Evelyn Brooks Higginbotham, "African-American Women's History and the Metalanguage of Race," *Signs* 17 (Winter 1992): 254-74; and Paula Giddings, *When and Where I Enter: The Impact of Black Women on Race and Sex in America* (New York: William Morrow & Company, 1996; orig. 1984).

[54] Karen Baker-Fletcher, *A Singing Something: Womanist Reflections on Anna Julia Cooper* (New York: Crossroad Publishing, 1994), 33-34, 35-36, 39, 48, 52-57; and Kevin K. Gaines, *Uplifting the Race: Black Leadership, Politics, and Culture in the Twentieth Century* (Chapel Hill: University of North Carolina, 1996), Chapter 5.

[55] *"...to be a woman of the Negro race in America..."* Anna Julia Cooper, *A Voice from the South: By a Black Woman of the South* (Xenia, OH: Aldine Publishing House, 1892), in Charles Lement and Esme Bhan, eds., *The Voice of Anna Julia Cooper* (Lanham, MD: Rowman & Littlefield, 1998), 113, 117.

[56] *"...is not for the little fellow..."* Cooper, "Equality of Races and the Democratic Movement," in Lement and Bhan, eds., *Voice of Anna Julia Cooper*, 297.

WALKING BY FAITH

[63] Kevin K. Gaines, *Uplifting the Race: Black Leadership, Politics, and Culture in the Twentieth Century* (Chapel Hill: University of North Carolina Press, 1996); and Robin D. G. Kelley, *Race Rebels: Culture, Politics, and the Black Working Class* (New York: The Free Press, 1994).

[65] *"...two women of the laboring classes..."* "Saturday Night and the Negro," *Washington Tribune*, 23 March 1928, 10.

Jacqueline M. Moore, *Leading the Race: The Transformation of the Black Elite in the Nation's Capital, 1880–1920* (Charlottesville: University Press of Virginia, 1999), 51-69, 161-86.

"...of the sororities..." Marcia M. Greenlee, Interview with Edward Feggans [Transcript], 19 September 1983, *Oral History Project*, Washingtoniana Division, D. C. Public Library, Washington, DC, 69-70.

[66] *"There was no question at that time..."* Collins Interview with Felicia E. Chisley [Transcript], 13 October 1995, Washington, DC, 9.

[67] Mary Church Terrell, "History of the High School for Negroes in Washington," *Journal of Negro History* 2 (July 1917): 252-66; and Douglass Pielmeier, "Roscoe Conkling Bruce and the District of Columbia's Public Schools, 1906 to 1921" (M.A. Thesis, University of Maryland, 1992).

"Within Dunbar, there was a kind of class..." Collins Interview with Chester and Enez Martin [Transcript], 13 October 1995, Washington, DC, 16-17; and Greenlee Interview with James and Barbara Walker [Transcript], 10 November 1983, 147-48.

"...from above and descend until it met..." Richard T. Stokes, *An Historical Analysis of Afro-American Higher Education With Special Emphasis on the Educational Ideas of Kelly Miller* (M. A. Thesis, Howard University, 1974), 32; Kelly Miller, "Forty Years of Negro Education," *Educational Review* 36 (June-December 1908): 484-98; "National Responsibility for the Education of the Negro," *Educational Review* 58 (June-December 1919): 31-38; "Education of the Negro in the North," *Educational Review* 62 (October 1921): 232-38; "The Harvest of Race Prejudice," *Survey Graphic* 53 (March 1925): 682-83, 711-12; "The Economic Plight of the Negro Demands Relentless Opposition [Editorial]," *Washington Tribune*, 5 October 1933, 4. "Is the City Negro Doomed? [Editorial]," *Washington Tribune*, 23 December 1932, 4; and Earl Ofari Hutchinson, *Blacks and Reds: Race and Class in Conflict, 1919–1990* (East Lansing: Michigan State University Press, 1995), 109.

[69] *"The Black population in Washington increased..."* Elizabeth Clark-Lewis, "'This Work Had a' End': African-American Domestic Workers in Washington, D.C., 1910–1940," in Carol Groneman and Mary Beth Norton, eds., *"To Toil the Livelong Day": America's Women At Work* (Ithaca: Cornell University Press, 1987), 196-99; and U. S. Department of Interior, Census Bureau, *Thirteenth*

Census of the United States, Volume II (Washington: Government Printing Office, 1913), Tables 1 and 4, 291; U. S. Department of *Commerce, Fourteenth Census of Population Characteristics of States, Volume III* (Washington: GPO, 1923), Table I, 178; *Fifteenth Census, Population: Volume III, Part I* (Washington: GPO, 1932), Table I, 385; and *Sixteenth Census*, Volume II, (Washington: GPO, 1943), Table 2, 956; and U. S. Department of Commerce, Census Bureau, *Fifteenth Census of the United States: 1930, Occupation Statistics, District of Columbia*, Table 11 (Washington: Government Printing Office, 1931), 11-13. See also: Elizabeth Clark-Lewis, *Living In, Living Out: African American Domestics in Washington, D. C., 1910–1940* (Washington: Smithsonian Institution Press, 1994).

"…protested with their feet…" James R. *Grossman, Land of Hope: Chicago, Black Southerners, and the Great Migration* (Chapel Hill: University of North Carolina Press, 1989).

[70] David Levering Lewis, *When Harlem Was in Vogue*; Grossman, *Land of Hope*; Peter Gottlieb, *Making Their Own Way: Southern Blacks' Migration to Pittsburgh, 1916–1930* (Pittsburgh: University of Pittsburgh Press, 1986); Robin D. G. Kelley, *Hammer and Hoe: Alabama Communists During the Great Depression* (Chapel Hill: University of North Carolina Press, 1990); Earl Lewis, *In Their Own Interests: Race, Class, and Power in Twentieth-Century Norfolk* (Berkeley: University of California Press, 1991), and Lawrence Otis Graham, *Our Kind of People: Inside America's Black Upper Class* (New York: HarperCollins, 1998).

Records of the Board of Education of the District of Columbia [RBEDC], 1934 (Washington: GPO, 1935), 59-60; *RBEDC, 1938* (Washington: GPO, 1938), 35-36.

[71] "Grave Situation Created in 1933 Bldg. Program," *Washington Tribune*, 12 February 1932, 9; "Excavating For New Vocational School For Boys," *Washington Tribune*, 31 March 1933, 9; "Kindergarten to College Proposed For Northeast," 16 March 1935, 9; Florence M. Collins, "One Additional Building Asked for Div. 11 Schools," *Washington Afro-American*, 23 May 1936, 12; and "Anacostia to Get New Housing Development," *Washington Afro-American*, 9 September 1939, 7.

Florence M. Collins, "Glaring Inequalities in 5-Year School Program," *Washington Afro-American*, 18 April 1936, 12; "Morgan School Transferred to Division

10," 17 January 1930, 2. See also: *RBEDC*, 1931–32 (Washington: GPO, 1932), 43-50, 58.

RBEDC, 1934 (Washington: GPO, 1934), 17; 1935, 17; 1936, 22; 1937, 19; 1938, 21; 1939, 22; and 1940, 26; "Schools Face Fund Cut," *Washington Afro-American*, 7 March 1936, 1; and "Senate Upsets Proportion of School Funds," 2 May 1936, 15; and Howard H. Long, "The Support and Control of Public Education in the District of Columbia," *Journal of Negro Education* 7 (July 1938): 390-99. See also: Austin D. Swanson and Richard A. King, *School Finance: Its Economics and Politics* (New York: Longman Press, 1991).

73 *"The entire colored school system was the best..."* Garnet C. Wilkinson, "Washington is Easily the Foremost Center of Negro Education in America," *School Life* 9 (February 1926): 114; "Wilkinson Sees Collapse in Fundamental Values," *Washington Afro-American*, 2 April 1938, 5.

Nathan I. Huggins, *Harlem Renaissance* (New York: Oxford University Press, 1971); and David L. Lewis, *When Harlem Was in Vogue* (New York: Oxford University Press, 1989).

75 "Randall Junior High School," in "Public School Notes," *Washington Tribune*, 1 February 1934, 11; "Public School Notes," 22 February 1934, 11; and "Proposes Art Galleries in High Schools," 1 February 1934, 1.

"Public School Notes," *Washington Tribune*, 22 February 1934, 11.

"Armstrong High School," in "Public School Notes," *Washington Tribune*, 5 April 1934, 10; *Occupation Statistics: District of Columbia* (Washington, 1931), Tables 11, 13; and M. M. Manring, *Slave in a Box: The Strange Career of Aunt Jemima* (Charlottesville: University Press of Virginia, 1998).

76 *"...interest in the communities has grown steadily..."* "Community Center Sponsors History Week Programs," *Washington Tribune*, 16 February 1935, 11; and "Dunbar Center Exhibits Dolls of Varied Types," *Washington Afro-American*, 29 January 1938, 12.

77 "YWCA News," *Washington Tribune*, 16 February 1935, 11. Note, too, that a number of White scholars in New York and Washington were simultaneously organizing interracial and international programs like the one at the Phyllis Wheatley YWCA in their "Intercultural Education" movement. For more about

this movement and its almost total exclusion of Blacks and other non-White groups, see: Nicholas Montalto, *A History of the Intercultural Education Movement, 1924–1941* (New York: Garland Publishing, 1982).

"Negro History Program To Be Given At Church," *Washington Tribune*, 22 April 1932, 10; "Thousands Drawn to Negro History Week Programs," *Washington Tribune*, 2 November 1933, 16; "Of What Service Are Our Schools," *Washington Tribune*, 29 January 1932, 10; Drusilla Dunjee Houston, "Taking Negro History To The Masses," 22 September 1934, 2; "Dunbar Center Exhibits Dolls of Varied Types," *Washington Afro-American*, 29 January 1938, 12; "Centers Ready to Celebrate History Week," *Washington Afro-American*, 5 February 1938, 3; and "D.C. Teachers to Hold History Week Seminar," 5 February 1938, 3. The Dunbar Center doll exhibit, ironically enough, paraded a host of White dolls and few, if any, dolls of Blacks. While this issue was not raised by observers or participants in 1938, by the end of the 1940s, with the work of Kenneth Clark and other Black scholars, the issue of skin color and inferiority regarding inter- and intrarace relations would begin to loom large in the desegregation strategy.

[78] *"Keep Abreast With the Time"* The Class of 1932, Dunbar High School, *Liber Anni 1932* (Washington: Dunbar High School, 1932), 67, in Charles Sumner School Museum and Archives, D.C. Public Schools; and "Washington Educators: An Intimate Series on the People Who Train Your Children," *Washington Afro-American*, 28 October 1939, 15.

"...were put over with a success." Thelma Lane and Louise Pinkett, "The Junior NAACP of Washington, D.C.," Letter to the National Office, no date, 1930s, in *NAACP Papers*, Container II-L 4, Library of Congress Manuscript Division, 3.

[79] *"All those things were instilled in us..."* Lane and Pinkett, Letter to National Office, 1-3; Collins Interview with Felicia E. Chisley [Transcript], 13 October 1995, 11, 15.

"If...somebody...mention[ed] the airbrake..." Collins Interview with Chester and Enez Martin [Transcript], 13 October 1995, 18-19; Greenlee Interview with James and Barbara Walker [Transcript], 10 November 1983, 147-48.

[81] *"...emphasize the Negro first, in the United States..."* "Kelly Miller Museum Program Wins Friends," *Washington Afro-American*, 2 July 1938, 5; and Janette

Hoston Harris, "Charles Harris Wesley, Educator and Historian, 1891–1947" (Ph.D. Dissertation: Howard University, 1975), 55-56.

"Kelly Miller Museum Program Wins Friends," *Washington Afro-American*, 2 July 1938, 5; Alain Locke, Letter to The President and the Board of Trustees, Howard University, 21 September 1938, 4, in *Alain L. Locke Papers*, Box 164-105, Moorland-Spingarn Research Center, Howard University; and Arthur J. Smith, "Praises Afro for 'Crashing' Library of Congress Files [Letter to the Editor]," *Washington Afro-American*, 11 September 1937, 3.

"H. U. to Observe History Week," *Washington Tribune*, 8 February 1934, 11; Mrs. McGuire H. U. League Speaker," 2 February 1935, 16.

"...the group needs education and economic sufficiency..." "Mrs. McGuire H. U. League Speaker," 2 February 1935, 16.

LOOKING FORWARD TO THE PAST

[87] *"...Black folks work for and White folks grant..."* Derrick A. Bell, *Faces At the Bottom of the Well: The Permanence of Racism* (New York: Basic Books, 1992), 18.

Michael Eric Dyson, *I May Not Get There With You: The True Martin Luther King, Jr.* (New York: Free Press, 2000), 290-95. Dyson examines the issue of "cultural amnesia" among both Whites and Blacks regarding the legacy of Martin Luther King and the Civil Rights movement, breaking down cultural amnesia into five categories: revisionist amnesia, reverential amnesia, repentant amnesia, recalcitrant amnesia, and resistant amnesia.

[88] Memorandum from Martin D. Jenkins to Attorney Leon A. Ransom, "Deficiencies in the Program of Browne Junior High School, Washington, D. C.," February 1947, 1, 2-5, in *NAACP—D. C. Branch Papers*, Box 78-44, Folders 865-873, Moorland-Spingarn Research Collection, Howard University; William Allyn Hill, "Presentation of the Statement of Findings and Conclusions of Educational Specialists on the Proposed Transfer of Five School Buildings from Divisions 1-9 to Divisions 10-13," 1947, 1-4; and "Statement of William A. Hill, Executive Secretary, District of Columbia Branch, National Association for the Advancement of Colored People to the House Sub-Committee on Appropriations," April 1948, 1-3, in *NAACP—D. C. Branch Papers*, Box 78-44, Folders

865-873, Moorland-Spingarn Research Collection, Howard University; "School Suits Before Court," *Washington Afro-American*, 11 December 1948, 1-2; "Let the Courts Decide [Editorial]," 11 October 1947, 6; and "Board Approves School Transfer by 7-2 Vote," 22 November 1947, 1, 26, in *Browne Junior High School and Carr Folder*, Washingtoniana Division, D. C. Public Library, Washington, D. C.; Letter from Hill to Senate Sub-Committee on District Revenue, 24 May 1948, 1-2, in *NAACP—D. C. Branch Papers*, Box 78-44, Folders 865-873, Moorland-Spingarn Research Collection, Howard University; and Constance M. Green, *The Secret City: A History of Race Relations in the Nation's Capital* (Princeton: Princeton University Press, 1967), 302-303.

Letter from Ernesto Galarza to Elise Watkins, 3 April 1947, 1-3; "White Girl in Colored School To Fight Transfer by Board," *Washington Evening Star*, April 1947; and Statement for Press from Ernesto Galarza, 14 April 1947, 1, in *Browne Junior High School and Carr Folder*, Washingtoniana Division, D. C. Public Library, Washington, D. C.

[89] *"Humorless…"* Letter from William Allyn Hill to Superintendent Corning, 25 September 1947, 1; "'Black Sambo' Story Use Protested," *Washington Post*, 27 September 1947; "Pros and Cons Pop Around Little Black Sambo, Still 'Just a Story' to Child," *Washington Post*, 28 September 1947, A-1; "'Black Sambo' Story Defended by Corning As No Racial Issue," *Washington Evening Star*, 27 September 1947, A-11; "Little Black Sambo [Editorial]," *Washington Post*, 30 September 1947; Sylvia M. Means, "'Little Black Sambo' [Letter to the Editor]," *Washington Post*, 1 October 1947; Woody L. Taylor, "'Little Sambo' Story Defended," *Washington Afro-American*, 4 October 1947, 1, 3; Ralph Matthews, "'Little Black Sambo': An Editorial," *Washington Afro-American*, 4 October 1947, 1-2; V. J. Dozier, "'Little Black Sambo' [Letter to the Editor]," *Washington Post*, 6 October 1947, 7; "'I'm Not Insulted,' Says Howard Prof," *Washington Afro-American*, 11 October 1947, 1, 22; and Matthews, "Emancipated Soul: An Editorial," 4 in *Little Black Sambo Folder*, Washingtoniana Division, D. C. Public Library, Washington, D.C.

[90] Carolivia Herron, *Nappy Hair* (New York: Random House, 1997); Lynette Holloway, "Teacher Threatened Over Book Weighs Switching Schools," *The New York Times*, 27 November 1998; Liz Leyden, "'Nappy Hair' Uproar Discourages Teacher," *Milwaukee Journal-Sentinel*, 13 December 1998, 27; and Tina Kelley, "After Furor Over Book, A Welcome Epilogue," *The New York Times*, 14 May 2000, A33.

[91] *"White flight"* and *"Black migration"* Sixteenth Decennial Census of the United States, Census of Population, 1940, (Washington: GPO, 1943), Volume II, Table 2, 956, *Part 3: Kansas-Michigan*, Table 21, 537, and *Part 7: Utah-Wyoming*, Table 22, 173, 177; *Seventeenth Decennial Census of the United States, Census of Population: 1950, Volume II, Part 9* (Washington, 1952), Table 9, 9-5, *Part 20*, Table 42, 20-55, and *Part 46*, Table 42, 46-95, 46-96; and *Eighteenth Decennial Census of the United States, Census of Population: 1960, Volume I, Part 10* (Washington, 1961), Tables 13 and 15, 10-11, *Part 22*, Table 28, 22-60, and *Part 48*, Table 28,48-110, 48-111.

[92] *"One half of the schools desegregated in 1954..."* Martha Shollenberger Swaim, "Desegregation in the District of Columbia Public Schools" (M. A. Thesis, Howard University, 1971), 140-42, 144-46; and Green, *Secret City*, 303-304, 308-10.

Beverly Elaine Reid, "Desegregation of the Public Schools of the District of Columbia, 1954–1959" (M. A. Thesis, Howard University, 1971), 40-41; and Roger W. Allen, "A Summary of Twentieth Century Economic Development of the District of Columbia and the Washington Metropolitan Area," *Records of the Columbia Historical Society* 51 (1975), 554-55.

[93] *"Caesar"* and *"Uncle Tom..."* Steven J. Diner, "Crisis of Confidence: Public Confidence in the School's of the Nation's Capital in the Twentieth Century," *Urban Education* 25 (July 1990), 120; and Barbara A. Sizemore, *The Ruptured Diamond: The Politics of the Decentralization of the District of Columbia Public Schools* (Washington: University Press of America, 1981), Table 3, 91.

[94] *"Large numbers of pupils enter the junior high school system ill-prepared..."* Diner, "Crisis of Confidence," 120-31; George D. Strayer, *Report of a Survey of the Public Schools of the District of Columbia, conducted under the auspices of the chairmen of the subcommittees on District of Columbia appropriations of the respective appropriations committees of the Senate and House* (Washington: Government Printing Office, 1949); and Carl F. Hansen, *Danger in Washington: The Story of My Twenty Years in the Public Schools in the Nation's Capital* (West Nyack, NY: Parker Publishing, 1968), 91-105, 197-99.

[95] Christopher Jencks, *Inequality: A Reassessment of the Effect of Family and Schooling in America* (New York: Harper & Row, 1972); David Tyack, *The One Best System: A History of American Urban Education* (Cambridge: Harvard University

Press, 1974); and Jeannie Oakes, *Keeping Track: How Schools Structure Inequality* (New Haven: Yale University Press, 1985).

97 *"...alternative to a 'Black Anglo-Saxon Mentality'..."* James Clark Moone, "The Problem of Designing an African-American Studies Program in U.S. Public Schools: The Challenge for New Directions 'A Case Study of the Washington, D.C. Public Schools, 1969–1974'" (Ph.D. Dissertation, Howard University, 1976), 112, 122-23; and New School of Afro-American Thought, "By-Laws and Organizations," 14 November 1967.

98 Jonathan I. Z. Agronsky, *Marion Barry: The Politics of Race* (New York: British American Publishing, 1990); and Jonetta Rose Barras, *The Last of the Black Emperors* (New York: Bancroft Press, 1998).

"Create love in the community..." Moone, "The Problem of Designing an African-American Studies Program," 96, 129, 131, 194-95; Louise Casandra Bailey, "Viewpoints of Negro Parents of Low Socio-Economic Levels Regarding the School and Education" (M. A. Thesis, Howard University, 1967), 46; Jacquelyn Stewart Clemons, "American History As Taught Through A Black Perspective: for use in the Elementary School" (M. A. Thesis, Howard University, 1972), 60; Janice Evelyn Carroll, "Teaching Non-Western Literature to High School Students" (M. A. Thesis, Howard University, 1969), 3; Dirk Anthony Ballendorf, "An Approach to the Teaching of History and Social Studies Curriculum Materials for the Disadvantaged" (M. A. Thesis, Howard University, 1965); Marie M. B. Racine, "Influence on Curriculum Development in the Public Schools of Washington, D.C., 1804–1982," in *Studies in D.C. History and Public Policy, Paper No. 4* (Washington: University of the District of Columbia, May 1982); Bobby Seale, *Seize the Time: The Story of the Black Panther Party and Huey P. Newton* (New York: Random House, 1970); Maurice R. Berube and Marilyn Gitell, *Confrontation at Ocean Hill-Brownsville: The New York School Strikes of 1968* (New York: Praeger, 1969); and Diane Ravitch, *The Great School Wars, New York City, 1805–1973: A History of the Public Schools as Battlefield of Social Change* (New York: Basic Books, 1974).

100 *"...superintendency began under a divisive racial cleavage..."* Hugh J. Scott, *The Black School Superintendent: Messiah or Scapegoat?* (Washington: Howard University Press, 1980), 87-102; and Barbara A. Sizemore, *The Ruptured Diamond: The Politics of the Decentralization of the District of Columbia Public Schools* (Washington: University Press of America, 1981), 142-44, 388-90, 398.

"...both sides have become so engrossed..." Sizemore, *Ruptured Diamond*, 438-39; and *Washington Post*, 3 May 1975, 13 August 1975.

[101] Diner, "Crisis of Confidence," 131-33.

[102] Rene Sanchez, "5-Year Plan Unveiled for District Schools," *Washington Post*, 22 June 1989, D1; Gary Putka, "Curricula of Color," *Wall Street Journal*, 1 July 1991, A4; Sari Horwitz, "D.C. Afrocentric Program in Trouble as Term Nears," *Washington Post*, 3 September 1993, B3; Horwitz, "Specialist Favors Expansion of District's Afrocentric Curriculum," 22 September 1994, A17; and Horwitz, "D.C. Schools Open Another Chapter on Afrocentrism," 21 February 1995, B1; DeNeen Brown, "Plotting a New Course for Education," *Washington Post*, 21 August 1995, B1; and Debbi Wilgoren, "Test Scores Get Conflicting Interpretations; School Officials, Parents Differ on Meaning of Improvements in Past 2 Years," *Washington Post*, 28 October 1999, J1.

Dorothy Gilliam, "Afrocentric Education Would Benefit All," *Washington Post*, 19 November 1990, B3; Lynda Richardson, "A New View from the Top: Franklin Smith's Agenda," *Washington Post*, 29 August 1991, J6; Sari Horowitz, "Unlicensed College Provided D.C. Afrocentric Training," *Washington Post*, 14 August 1993, A1; and Horowitz, "D.C. Afrocentric Program in Trouble as Term Nears: Deadline Is Today for Curriculum Revisions," *Washington Post*, 3 September 1993, B3.

[104] *"We abdicated responsibility, and we abdicated our strengths..."* Collins Interview with Felicia Chisley [Transcript], 13 October 1995, 17, 18, 19.

[105] *"...has to be with the Black community..."* Collins Interview with Donna Potts [Transcript], 17 November 1995, Washington, D.C., 17.

"...it's the cotton pickers running the city..." Jervis Anderson, "Our Far-Flung Correspondents: The Dunbar High School on First Street," *The New Yorker*, March 20, 1978, 93-121.

[106] *"We didn't just close up and die..."* Michel McQueen, "Dunbar Reunion: The Class of 1935 Looks Back On Years of Struggle, Success," *Washington Post*, 29 June 1980, B2.

[106] *"...go for the gusto..."* Greenlee Interview with Edward Feggans [Transcript], 19 September 1983, 87-89, 111.

[107] "...we were able to afford the better clubs..." Greenlee Interview with Edward Feggans [Transcript], 19 September 1983, 87-89, 111.

[109] *"Cultural amnesia"* Dyson, *I May Not Get There With You*, Chapters 9 and 13; Mary Patillo-McCoy, *Black Picket Fences: Privilege and Peril among the Black Middle Class* (Chicago: University of Chicago Press, 1999).

ULTIMATE FEAR REALIZED

[114] *"...as a static, measurable thing..."* Robin D. G. Kelley, *Yo' Mama's Disfunktional!: Fighting the Culture Wars in Urban America* (Boston: Beacon Press, 1997), 9, 17.

James A. Banks, ed., *Multicultural Education, Transformative Knowledge, and Action: Historical and Contemporary Perspectives* (New York: Teachers College Press, 1996); James A. Banks, *Multiethnic Education: Theory and Practice, 3rd ed.* (Boston: Allyn and Bacon, 1993); James A. Banks and Cherry A. McGee Banks, *Multicultural Education: Issues and Perspectives* (Boston: Allyn and Bacon, 1997); Christine E. Sleeter and Carl A. Grant, "An Analysis of Multicultural Education in the United States," *Harvard Educational Review* 57 (May 1987): 421-44; and Christine E. Sleeter, ed., *Empowerment through Multicultural Education* (Albany, NY: SUNY Press, 1991).

[115] Alfred J. Lindsey, "Consensus or Diversity? A Grave Dilemma in Schooling," *Journal of Teacher Education* 36 (July-August 1985): 31-39; Asa G. Hilliard, III, "Teachers and Cultural Styles in a Pluralistic Society," *NEA Today* 7 (January 1989): 65-69; Jeff Kleinhuizen, "Lessons From Many Cultures; Educators Strive For Diversity," *USA Today,* 20 February 1991, 7D; Erich Martel, "How Valid Are the Portland Baseline Essays?," *Educational Leadership* 49 (December 1991): 20-23; and John O'Neil, "On the Portland Plan: A Conversation with Matthew Prophet," *Educational Leadership* 49 (December 1991): 24-27.

[116] *"Melanin theory"* Frances Cress Welsing, *The Isis Papers: The Keys to the Colors* (Chicago: Third World Press, 1991).

"...the preponderant Eurocentric myths..." Molefi K. Asante, *The Afrocentric Idea* (Philadelphia: Temple University Press, 1987), 8-9; Maulana R. Karenga, *Introduction to Black Studies, 4th Edition* (Los Angeles: University of Sankore Press, 1987); and Karenga, ed., *Reconstructing Kemetic Culture: Papers, Perspectives,*

Projects (Los Angeles: University of Sankore Press, 1990); John Henrik Clarke, *African People in World History* (Baltimore: Black Classic Press, 1993); "African Dreams [Cover Story]," *Newsweek*, 23 September 1991; and Martin Bernal, *Black Athena: The Afroasiatic Roots of Classical Civilization, Volumes 1 and 2* (New Brunswick, NJ: Rutgers University Press, 1987/1991).

[117] Michael Eric Dyson, *Race Rules: Navigating the Color Line* (Reading, MA: Addison-Wesley, 1996).

"Egyptocentrism" Wilson Jeremiah Moses, *Afrotopia: The Roots of African American Popular History* (New York: Cambridge University Press, 1998), 6, 17.

[118] John Blake, "Taking Pride in Their Heritage: New Curriculum 'Infuses' African History into Other Subjects," *Atlanta Journal-Constitution*, 19 February 1990, C1; Atlanta Public Schools, "The African Infusion Project," September 1991; Dorothy Gilliam, "Giving African History Its Due," *Washington Post*, 16 April 1990, D3; and Gilliam, "Afrocentric Education Would Benefit All," 19 November 1990, B3; "Schools Put Focus On Africa," *Washington Post*, 17 May 1990, J3; "Milwaukee's Backward March," *Baltimore Sun*, 12 November 1990, 6A; and Curtis Lawrence, "School Board Panel Rejects End to Afrocentric Teaching," *Milwaukee Journal-Sentinel*, 4 December 1996, 1.

"Traditional education policies..." William J. Bennett, *Our Children and Our Country: Improving America's Schools and Affirming the Common Culture* (New York: Simon & Schuster, 1988), 52-53; Barbara Vobejda, "Bennett Assails New Stanford Program," *Washington Post*, 19 April 1988, A5.

[119] Sam Howe Verhovek, "Plan to Emphasize Minority Cultures Ignites A Debate," *New York Times*, 21 June 1991, A1, A3; Gary Putka, "Curricula of Color," *The Wall Street Journal*, 1 July 1991, A1, A4; Joseph Berger, "Arguing About America," *New York Times*, 21 June 1991; and New York State Education Department, *One Nation, Many Peoples: A Declaration of Cultural Interdependence* (Albany, NY: The Report of the New York State Social Studies Review and Development Committee, 1991).

[120] *"Openness" and "e pluribus plures"* Allan Bloom, *The Closing of the American Mind: How Higher Education Has Failed Democracy and Impoverished the Souls of Today's Students* (New York: Simon & Schuster, 1987), 34; Dinesh D'Souza, *Illiberal Education: The Politics of Race and Sex on Campus* (New York: Free Press, 1991), 81; and Diane Ravitch, "Multiculturalism: E Pluribus Plures," *American*

Scholar 59 (Summer 1990): 337-54. See also Ravitch, *Left Back: A Century of Failed School Reforms* (New York: Simon & Schuster, 2000), 408-53; and Jonathan Zimmerman, *Whose America: Culture Wars in the Public Schools* (Cambridge: Harvard University Press, 2002), 107-32.

[121] *"Not all efforts at introducing a multicultural curriculum...."* Bennett, *The De-Valuing of America: The Fight for Our Culture and Our Children* (New York: Summit Books, 1992), 194-95.

"Cult of ethnicity..." Arthur M. Schlesinger, Jr., *The Disuniting of America: Reflections on a Multicultural Society* (New York: W. W. Norton, 1992), 83; W. E. B. Du Bois, *Dusk of Dawn: An Essay Toward an Autobiography of a Race Concept* (New York: Harcourt, Brace, 1940), 116; Du Bois, *Writings* (New York: The Library of America, 1986), 639, 755; and Du Bois, "Not 'Separatism' [Editorial]," *Crisis* 19 (February 1919): 166. Note that this would not be the first time in Du Bois' life that his own statements would eventually contradict him (see Du Bois on segregation, *Crisis* 41 (January-June 1934), but it is safe to say that Du Bois never argued for full African American assimilation in American society.

[122] *"...emerged with a program of Pan-Africanism..."* Du Bois, *The Autobiography of W. E. B. Du Bois: A Soliloquy on Viewing My Life from the Last Decade of Its First Century* (New York: International Publishers, 1968), 289, 295.

[123] *"...part of the homosexual movement..."* Josh Barbanel, "Under 'Rainbow,' a War: When Politics, Morals and Learning Mix," *New York Times*, 27 December 1992, A34.

"Some blame for misconceptions lies with television and newspapers..." Steven Lee Myers, "How a 'Rainbow Curriculum' Turned Into Fighting Words," *New York Times*, 13 December 1992, D6; Joseph Berger, "Queens Board Rejects Fernandez Offer to Talk," *New York Times*, 16 December 1992, B2; "Conservatives Rain on 'Rainbow' Curriculum and Fernandez," *UPI*, 4 February 1993.

[124] *"Same gender"* Barbanel, "Fernandez Modifies Parts of Curriculum About Gay Parents," *New York Times*, 27 January 1993, A1; "'Same Gender' Replaces 'Gay'; N.Y.C. Rewrites Curriculum," *AP Wire*, 27 January 1993; Joseph Fernandez, "Linking Desegregation to Multicultural Education [Speech]," from *The 40th Anniversary of Brown v. Board of Education Conference*, 17 May 1994; and Jan Hoffman, "Ex-Chancellor Recalls His Turn on Hot Seat," *New York Times*, 13 May 1999.

[125] *"...the first milestone in the development of standards..."* National Council for History Standards, *National Standards for United States History: Exploring the American Experience* (Los Angeles: National Center for History in the Schools, 1994), iii.

[126] *"...an outline for the teaching of American history..."* Lynne V. Cheney, "The End of History," *Wall Street Journal*, 20 October 1994, A26; and Cheney, *Telling the Truth: Why Our Culture and Our Country Have Stopped Making Sense—and What We Can Do About It* (New York: Simon & Schuster, 1995); Guy Gugliotta, "Up in Arms About the 'American Experience,'" *Washington Post*, 28 October 1994, A3; Gary B. Nash, "On U.S. History Standards," *Historian* 57 (Winter 1995): 457-59; Jon Wiener, "History Lesson," *New Republic*, 2 January 1995, 9-11; George F. Will, "Give Them The Ax," *Washington Post*, 8 January 1995, C7; "Battling Over History," *Christian Science Monitor*, 30 January 1995, 18; John Leo, "History Standards Are Bunk," *U.S. News & World Report*, 6 February 1995) 23; Gary L. Bauer, "National History Standards: Clintonites Miss the Moon," *Family Research Council Perspectives*, http://www.frc.org (March 1995): 1-3; LynNell Hancock and Nina Biddle, "History Lessons," *Newsweek*, 10 July 1995,28-32; Newt Gingrich, "Cutting Cultural Funding: A Reply," *Time*, 21 August 1995, 70-71; Diane Ravitch and Arthur Schlesinger, Jr., "The New, Improved History Standards," *Wall Street Journal*, 3 April 1996, A1; and Michael Kammen, "Culture and the State in America," *Journal of American History* 83 (December 1996): 791-814.

[127] *"Can a plurality of stories and jarring perspectives..."* Gary B. Nash, Charlotte Crabtree, and Ross E. Dunn, *History on Trial: Culture Wars and the Teaching of the Past* (New York: Alfred A. Knopf, 1997), 101, 117-18; Nash, "The Great Multicultural Debate," *Contention* 1 (Spring 1992): 1-28.

[128] Debra Adams and Margaret Trimer-Hartley, "First Day Delights Most: Academy Opens Without Incident, Detroiters Cheerfully Cope with Chaos," *Detroit Free-Press* (30 September 1992), 1B; Lori Olszewski, "Oakland Residents Praise School Ebonics Plan: Support for Board Vote at Town Meeting," *San Francisco Chronicle* (9 January 1997), 1; and Cheryl D. Fields, "Ebonics 101: What Have We Learned?," *Black Issues in Higher Education* 13 (23 January 1997): 18-21, 24-28.

"...out of our many different strands one America..." President William J. Clinton, "One America in the 21st Century [Speech]," *www.Whitehouse.gov*, 14 June

1997; and The Advisory Board on Race, *One America in the 21st Century: Forging a New Future* (Washington: GPO, 1998), 1.

[129] *"...not a definitive analysis of the state of race relations in America today..."* Advisory Board on Race, *One America*, 10, 11, 12-17.

[130] *"...nothing to contribute."* Derrick Z. Jackson, "A Case of Discrimination—By Clinton's Race Panel," *Boston Globe*, 26 November 1997; "Dr. Franklin's One-Sided Dialogue, *Chicago Tribune*, 21 November 1997,; and Peter Baker and Thomas B. Edsall, "Clinton Initiative on Race Is Lacking, Gingrich Says," *Washington Post*, 21 November 1997, A16.

[132] *"I am a Scotch-Irish Southern Baptist..."* President Clinton, "One America," 3.

EPILOGUE

[135] *"...you get out of something profound..."* Jacques Steinberg, "After Bitter Campus Battles, The 'Great Books' Rise Again," *New York Times*, 18 January 2000, A1, A17.

[136] Locke, ed., *New Negro*; Vincent P. Franklin, *The Education of Black Philadelphia: The Social and Educational History of a Minority Community, 1900–1950* (Philadelphia: University of Pennsylvania Press, 1979); and Grossman, *Land of Hope*.

[138] See Gerald Grant and Christine E. Murray, *Teaching in America: The Slow Revolution* (Cambridge: Harvard University Press, 1999).

[139] "Right Women," *20/20* [ABC Newsmagazine], 12 July 2000.

Acknowledgments

In a work that requires a large measure of solitude, there are always those who enable the author of a manuscript such as this one to complete what is often an impossible task. As for me, without my God, none of this would have been possible. Overcoming my own fears in writing and publishing *Fear of a "Black" America* has required a power beyond my own. So I give thanks to my higher power, the One who created me and my ability to write this book.

I must also thank my former agent Claudia Menza, who pursued publishers for *Fear of a "Black" America* for more than three years. She cared deeply about my project, but had a difficult task as an agent who mostly represented fiction writers convincing nonfiction editors of my book's viability and profitability. In a similar vein, the editors who have reviewed *Fear of a "Black" America* deserve credit for encouraging me to shape the book into a hybrid between traditional academic nonfiction and a readable general audience work. I especially give thanks to Matthew Byrnie at Routledge, Amy Caldwell at Beacon Press, and Hilary Claggett at Greenwood/Praeger Books for their time and energy spent in reviewing the project, as well as for their encouraging responses. Although none of them could convince their editorial boards to publish my book, they at least felt that the project had a place in the publishing world.

On the academic side of things, several professors and educators served as key contributors to the direction of this project, especially in the introductions to each of the book's chapters. To Joe Trotter at Carnegie Mellon University, thanks for the revelation that I needed to make my own road as a writer and educator, as your mentorship proved unequal to the task of lighting my path. For Dan Resnick, who believed that I was a better writer than a scholar, thanks for enabling me to realize that I am a writer first and foremost, and that badly-written scholarship means nothing in the world outside of academia. Richard Altenbaugh at Slippery Rock University served as editor for manuscripts related to *Fear of a "Black" America*. Thanks, Dick, for allowing me to move in another, innovative direction as a writer by not publishing my manuscript in the *History of Education Quarterly*. To Bruce Anthony Jones, now at University of Missouri-Kansas City, thanks for the absence of your support for my book in its initial stages, as well as for the $100-loan in 1997. I truly hope that you have found your path as a non-teaching professor. But most of all in this group, I must extend thanks to Estelle Abel, a retired educator from Mount Vernon High School in New York. She made me realize long before I had ever considered a book on multicultural-ism that wisdom and age often do not mix. This is especially true in the context of elitism and race.

There have been other, more rewarding experiences on the path to completing and publishing this manuscript. I tortured my former students during my days at Carnegie Mellon, Duquense, and George Washington University with several chapters from *Fear of a "Black" America* in their earlier stages. Their comments, questions, and corrections have helped to make this book more responsive to the perspectives of teachers and students unfamiliar with the nuances of multicultur-alism or today's "culture wars" in the public schools. Most prominent among these students is Andrew Hartman, a promising history doctoral candidate at George Washington University. His editing and youthful inspiration helped me recapture some of my youth and inspiration in the final stages of this project.

I would be remiss if I did not acknowledge the assistance I received from archivists, librarians, and other professionals while working on *Fear of a "Black" America*. Among others, I thank: Roxanna Deane and the Washingtoniana Divi-sion of Martin Luther King Memorial Library, D. C. Public Library System; Anatol Steck and Ruby Herring of the Charles Sumner School Museum and Archives (D. C. Public Schools); the National Archives; the Library of Congress Manuscript and Geography and Map Divisions; the Moorland-Spingarn Research Collection at Howard University; Spencer Crew, now the Executive Director of the National Underground Railroad Freedom Center; and Caroline Stokes of the Columbia Historical Society for all their help in tracking down sources.

I must turn now to those whose life histories became significant sources in this book, for their memories added significant insights. With all sincerity, I thank Felicia Chisley, Chester and Enez Martin, and Donna Potts for making available their time, their homes, and their experiences for me and this project. Wherever they are, I hope that they know how much I appreciate their openness in sharing their stories with me.

A number of faculty and former graduate students listened to my gripes, gave me bits and pieces of advice, and helped steer me in directions that made the road to finishing smoother. I extend my appreciation to Adina Back, Carla Gary, C. Matthew Hawkins, John Hinshaw, Jonathan Holloway, Stephen Lewis, Edward Lomax, Susan McElroy, Richard Patz, Sandra Stein, and Carl Zimring,

One other venue of inspiration and advice for *Fear of a "Black" America* came from the New Voices Fellows that I worked with during my time as that program's assistant director. Their dedication to social justice in the U.S. and around the world gave me reason to continue working on a book that many editors said was important but out of step with our post-9/11 times. The responses of former New Voices Fellows to the idea of this book (as well as the manuscript itself), especially Christine Ahn, Denise McVea, Gin Pang, Terrance Pitts, Ian Urbina, and Olivia Wang, served as additional motivation.

There are those people who played significant roles in my life and in the process that deserve special thanks. In the days when I could not even pay rent, much less work on the project, when I did not know if I could write this book, and in my darkest hours as a struggling writer and recovering academician, these people were there for me as true friends and colleagues. With my deepest regards, I thank the late Harold Meltzer for his constant wisdom, his faith in my own faith and motivation, and for remaining the teacher and friend I came to know in high school. Even in the years after he retired, Mr. Meltzer revealed a world to me beyond myself, and an understanding of the human condition that many of us can only wish for. I will miss him and his wisdom, but I am thankful for having known him for eighteen years. Barbara Lazarus is another mentor whom I will miss, for she also had that rare combination of sincerity, wisdom, and caring that one would hope for in their parents or as a parent. She too, moved out of my life all too soon, but gave so much in helping me find my way as a writer and educator.

Lest I forget, several other friends, mentors, and colleagues have proven indispensable in enabling me to complete this book. To Yvonne Williams and Catherine Lacey, two people whom think the world of me, thanks for listening to my rants and cynicism, but not allowing me to be cynical. If it were not for people like Yvonne and Catherine, the world would be a place of utter hopelessness. To Catherine Lugg at Rutgers University and Marya McQuirter at the Humanities Council of Washington, DC, both of whom examined large chunks of my book in its early stages and remained my friends despite years passing without so much as a lunch together, I extend my appreciative thanks. Of course, I must also thank Marc Hopkins, James Lee, Carlton McLellan, and Sandy Weinbaum, who all directly or inadvertently pushed me to self-publish this book.

Last but not least, I need to thank loved ones for their help and encouragement in pushing me to finish this project. To Angelia, my wife, lover, friend, editor, and task master, I thank you for your inspiration, faith, prodding, critical analysis, and patience throughout this long journey. She has been Samwise Gamgee to my Frodo Baggins, and without her I would have given up on a writing career years ago. To her I give my most heartfelt, unequivocal thanks. To my son, Noah Michael, thanks for the last bit of inspiration that any father would need to publish a book. It is because I desire a better future for you, me, and for all of us that I have published *Fear of a "Black" America* now instead of later or never. I hope that when you are old enough to read this that you will understand the meaning of these words.

About the Author

Donald Earl Collins is a freelance writer who has published on the relationship between multiculturalism and African Americans in *Black Issues in Higher Education*, *Gannett Suburban Newspapers*, *History of Education Quarterly*, *Pittsburgh Post-Gazette*, *The Washington Post*, and *Radical Society*. Although Dr. Collins describes himself as a "recovering academic," he has served as an adjunct professor at Carnegie Mellon and Duquesne University in Pittsburgh. Most recently, Dr. Collins was an adjunct professor in the Graduate School of Education and Human Development at George Washington University. Dr. Collins is also the Deputy Director of the Partnerships for College Access and Success Program at the Academy for Educational Development in New York and Washington, DC. Dr. Collins earned a doctorate in history from Carnegie Mellon University. He currently resides in Silver Spring, Maryland with his wife and son.

Index

0-595-32552-1

www.ingramcontent.com/pod-product-compliance
Lightning Source LLC
Chambersburg PA
CBHW021603280526
45784CB00001BA/476